MAJESTIC MANDALAS

Stress-Relieving Designs:

Mandalas, Flowers, Floral Patterns
And Decorative Designs

Adult Coloring Books

Katherine Pens

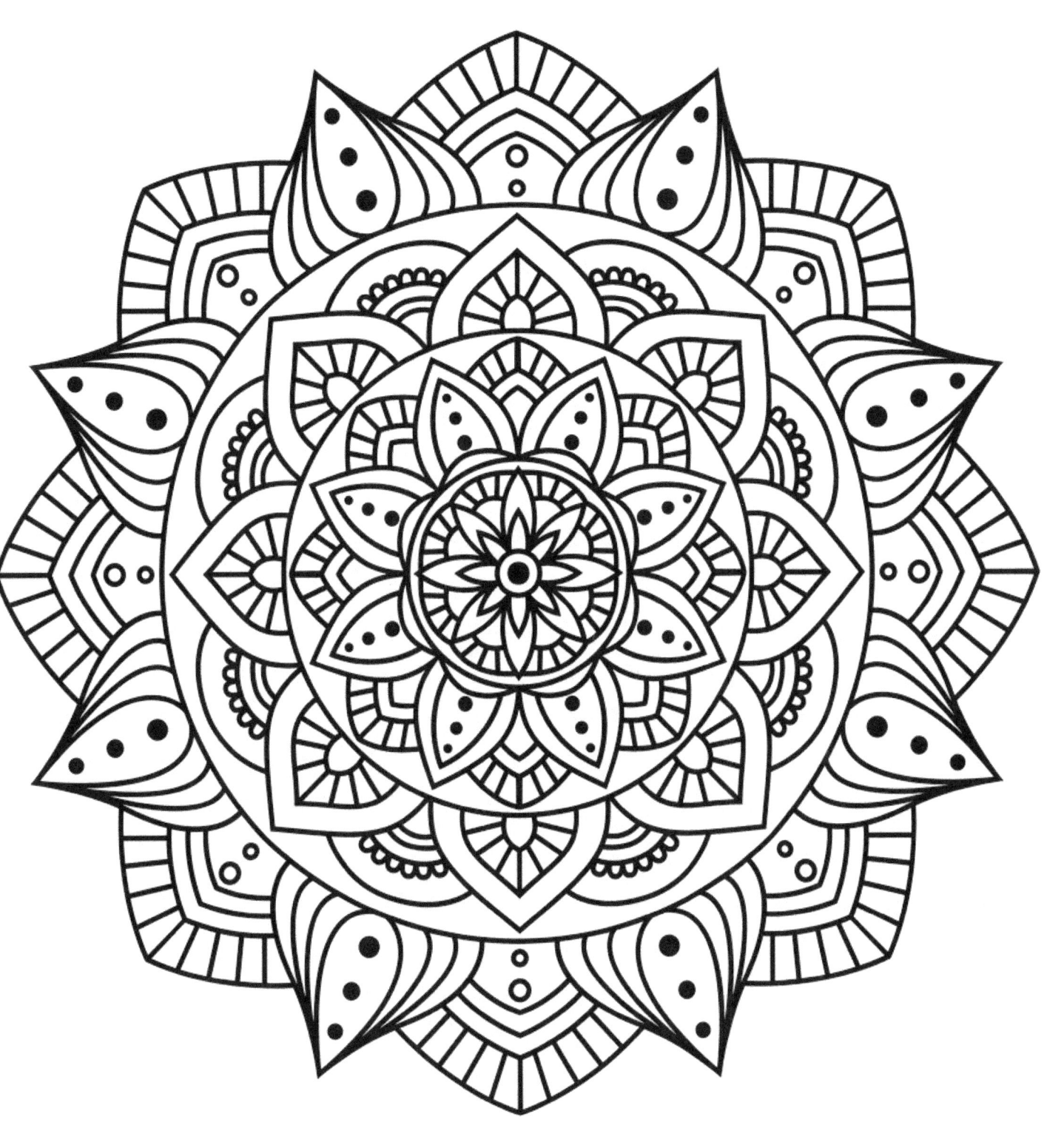

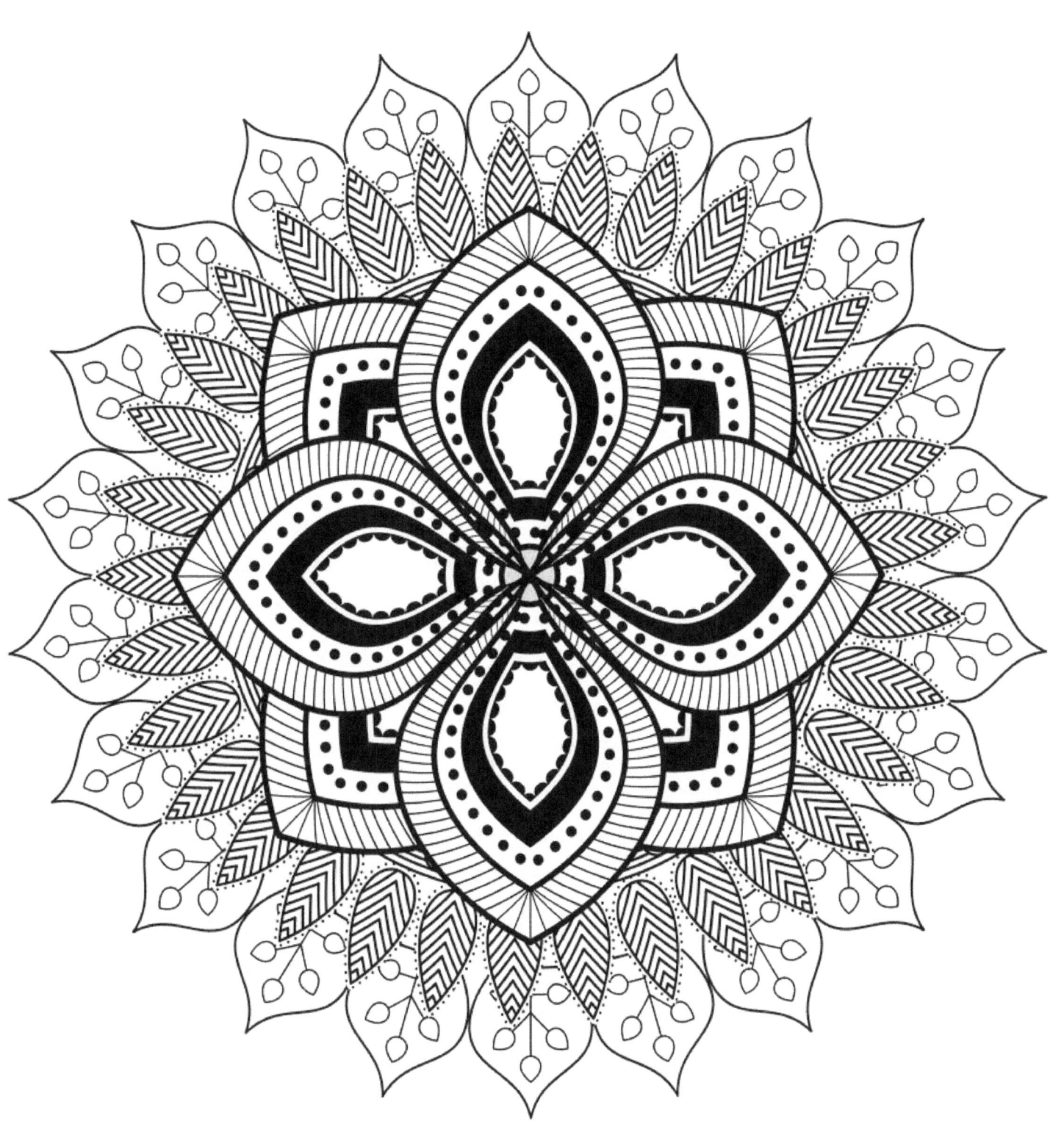

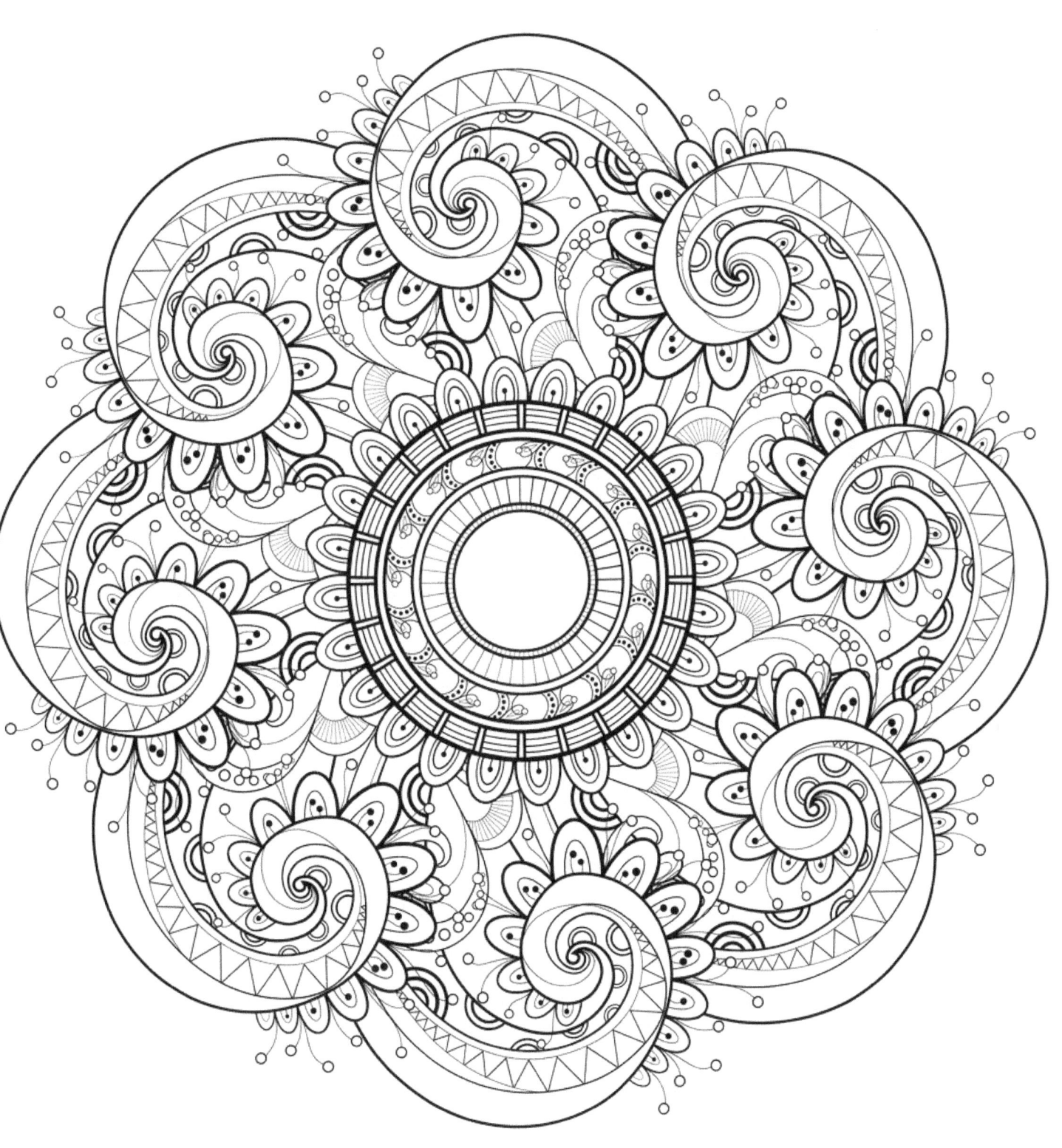

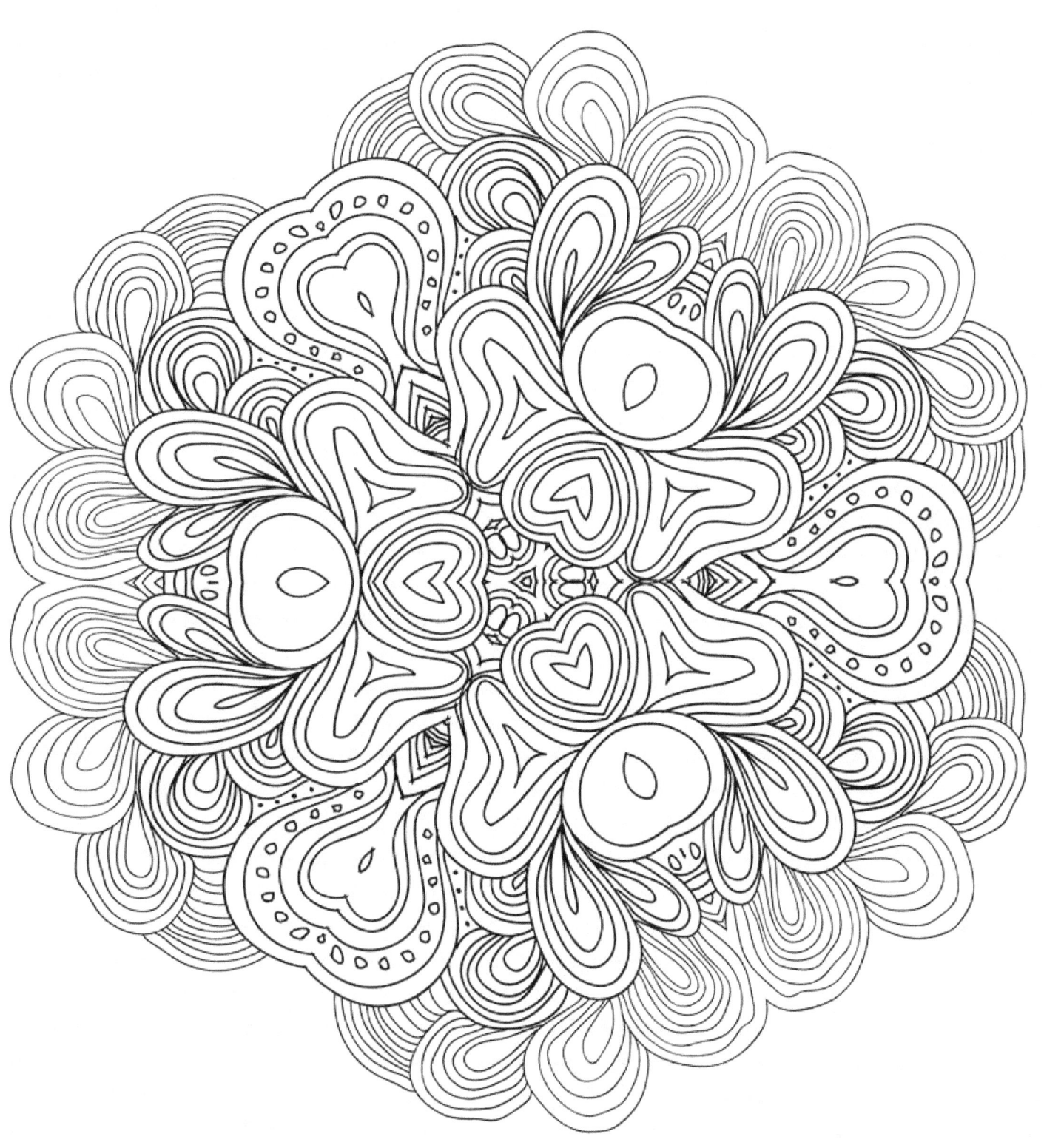

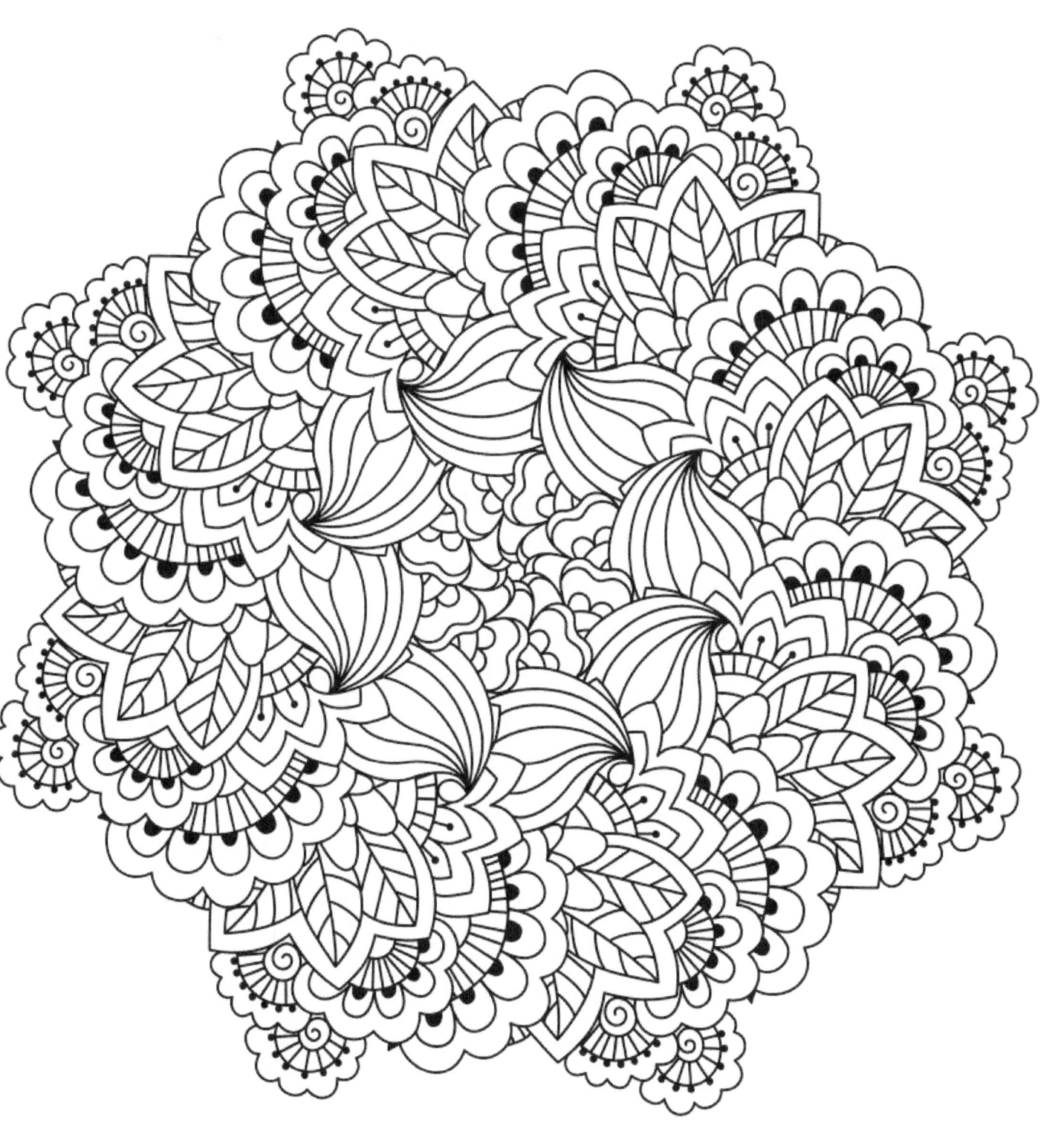

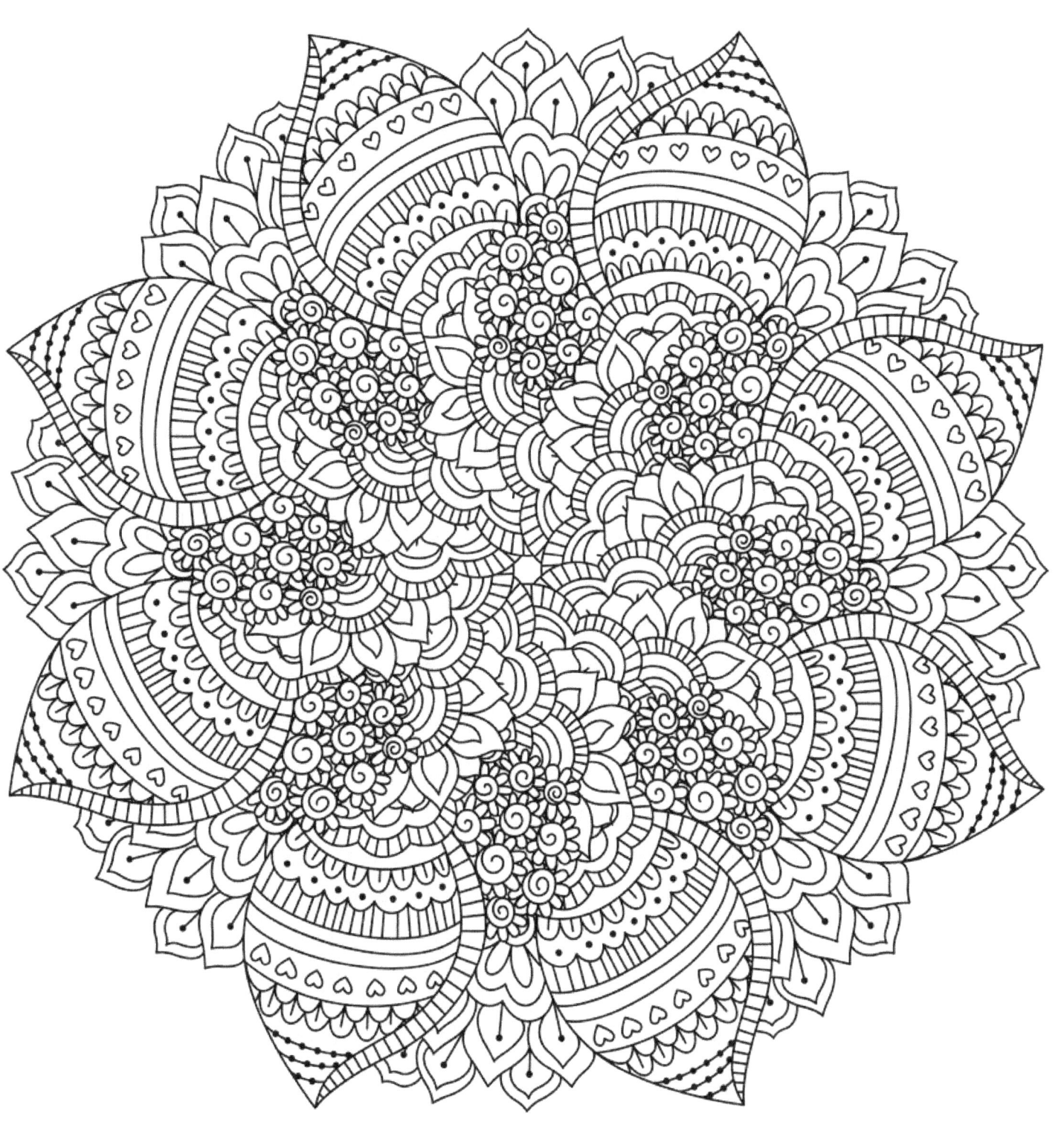

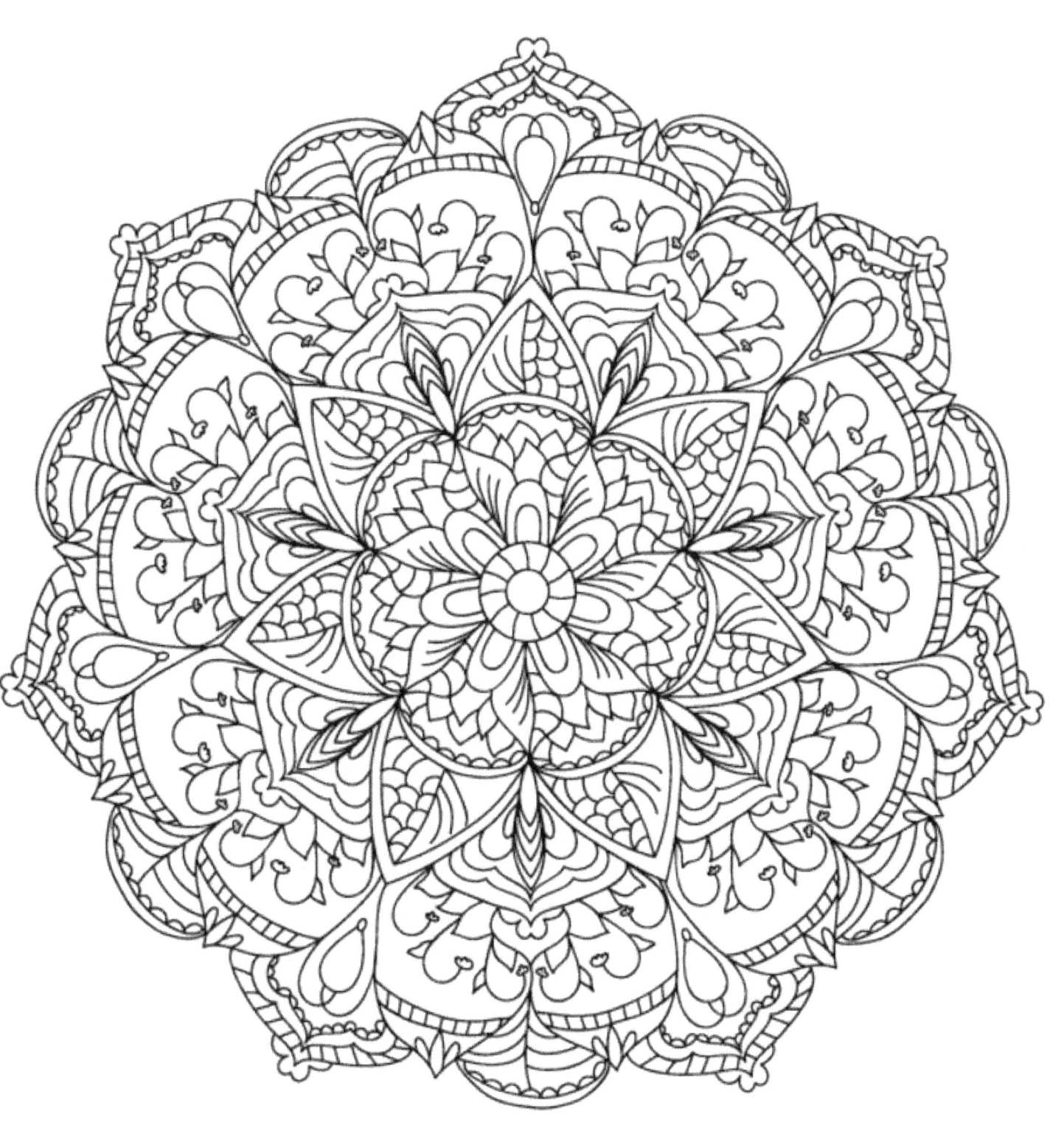

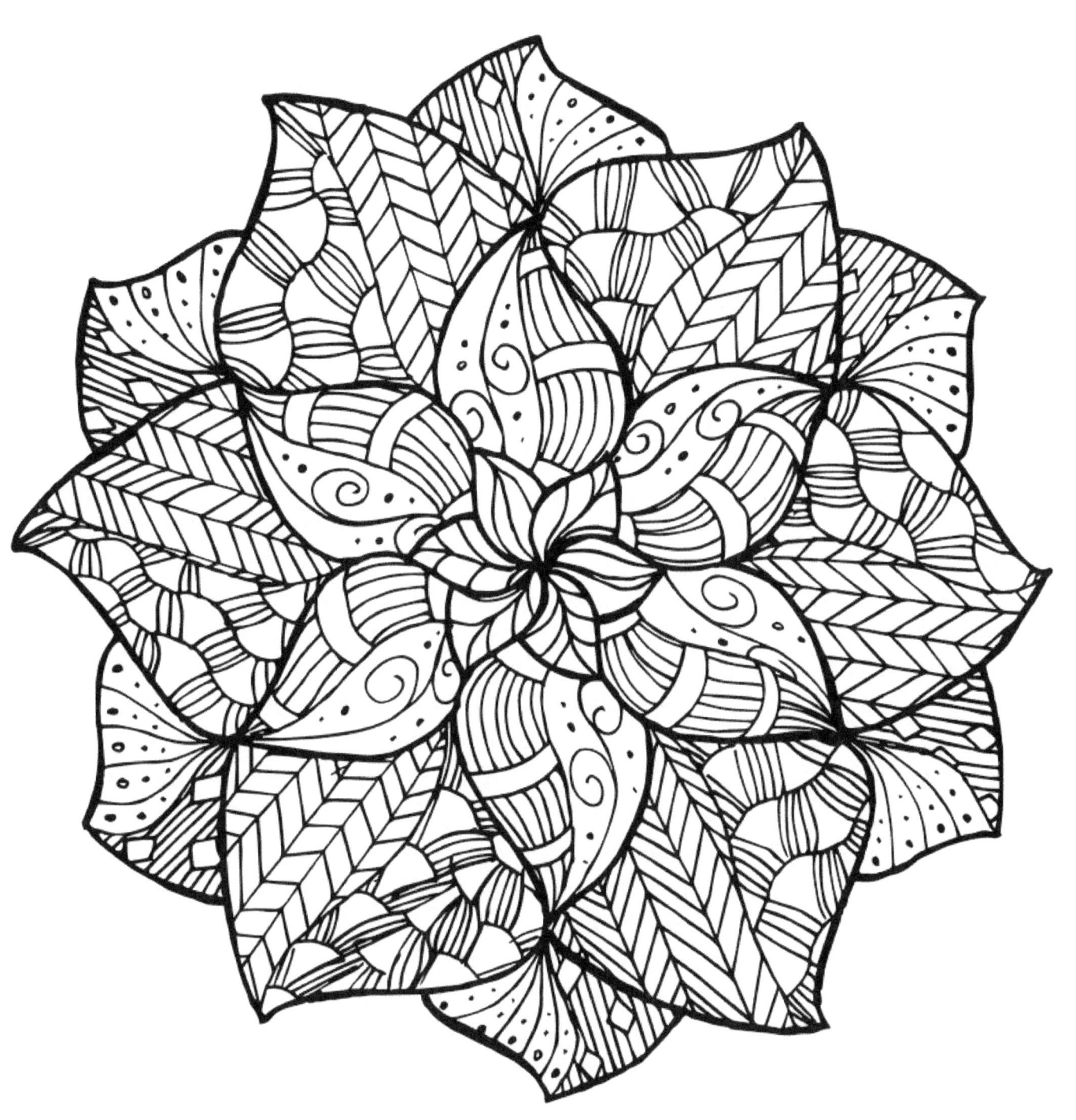

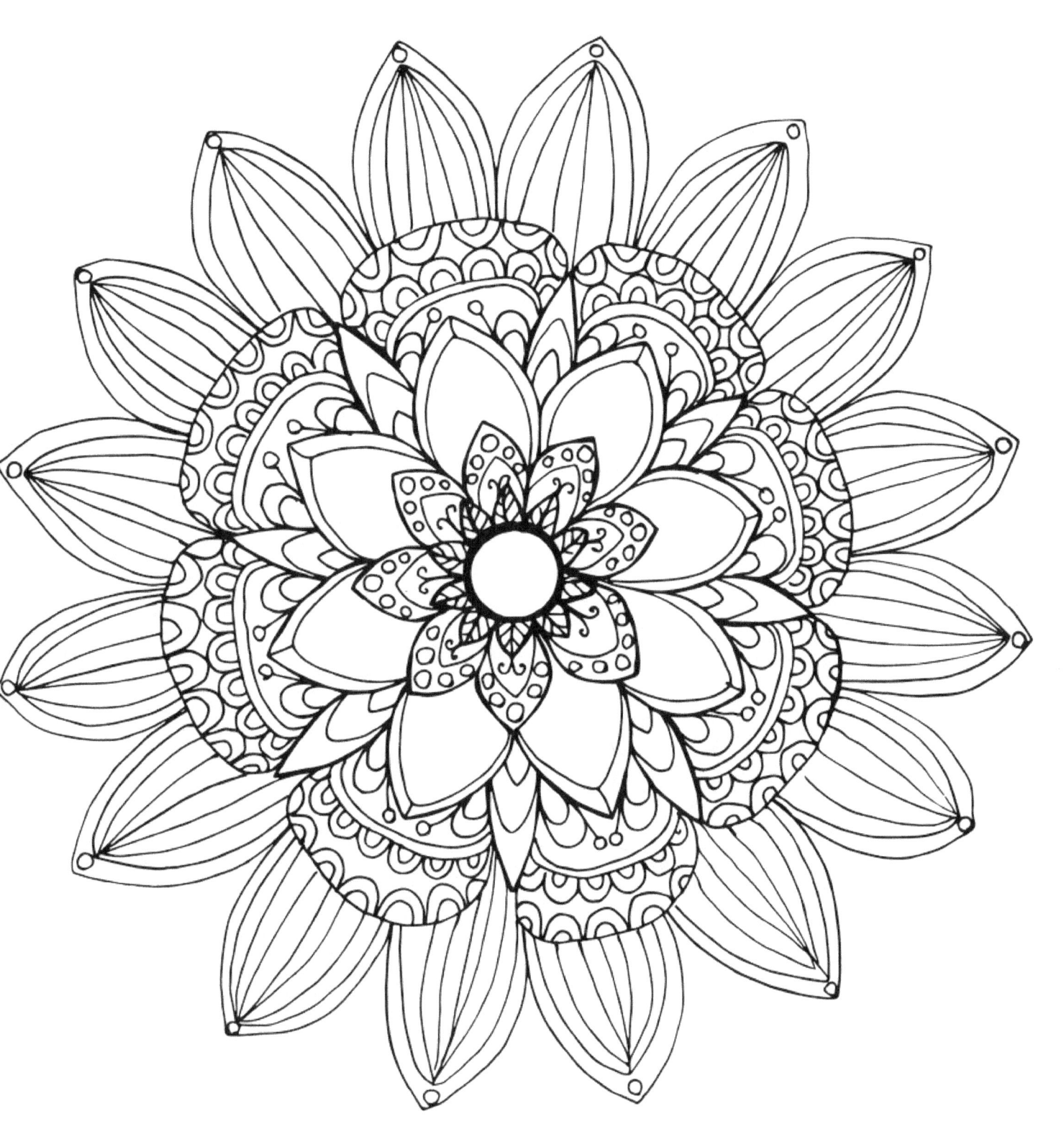

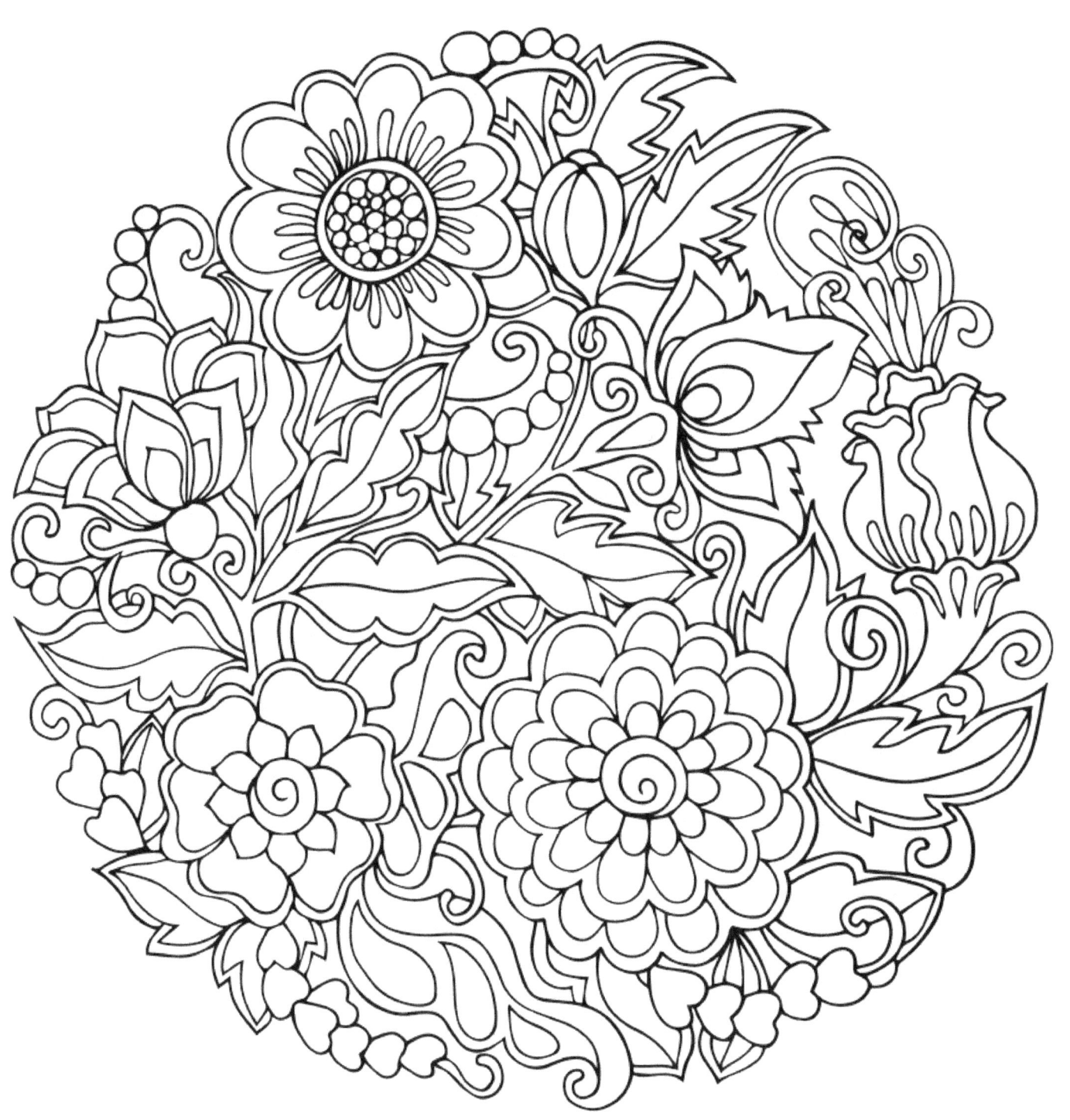

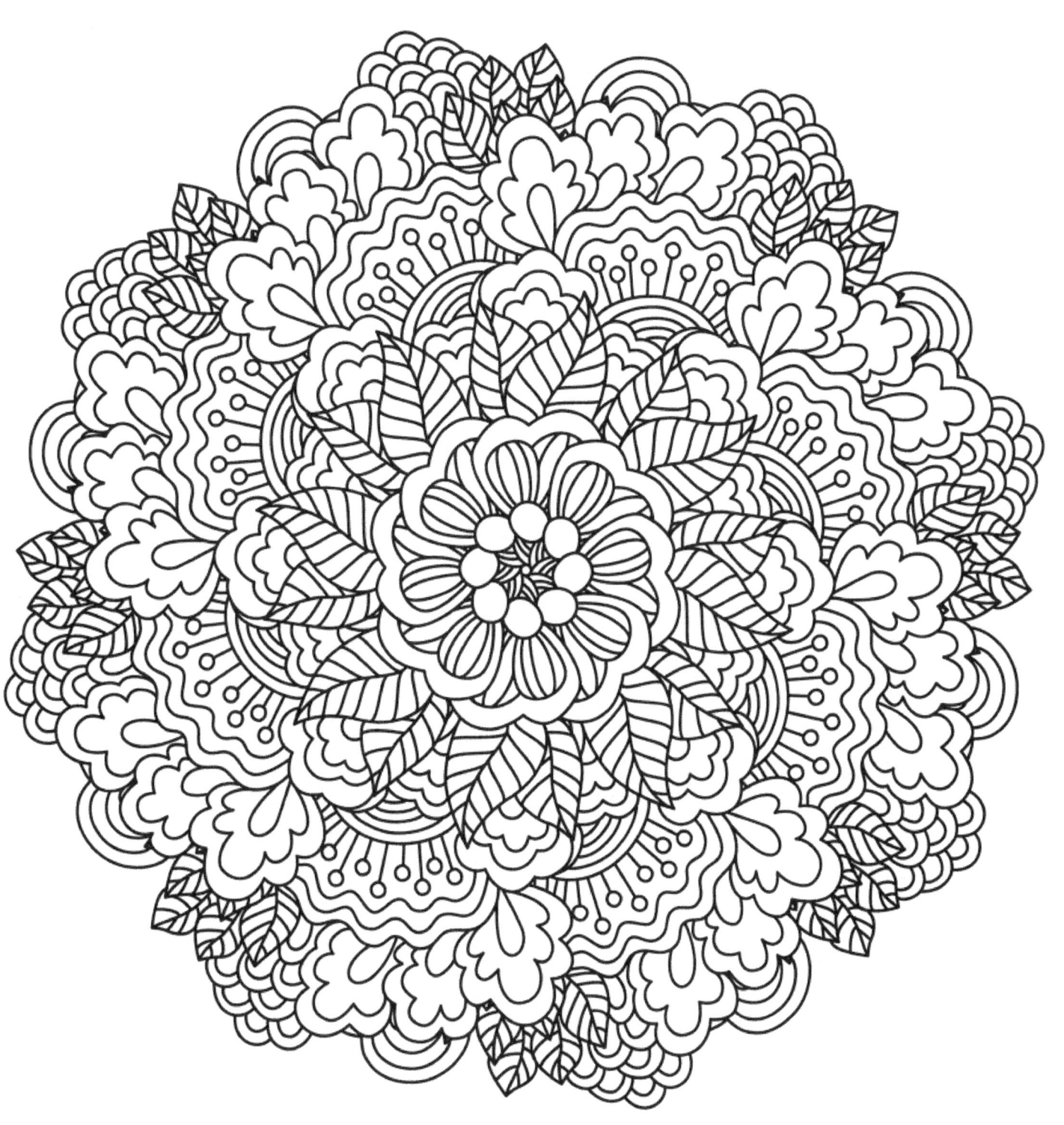

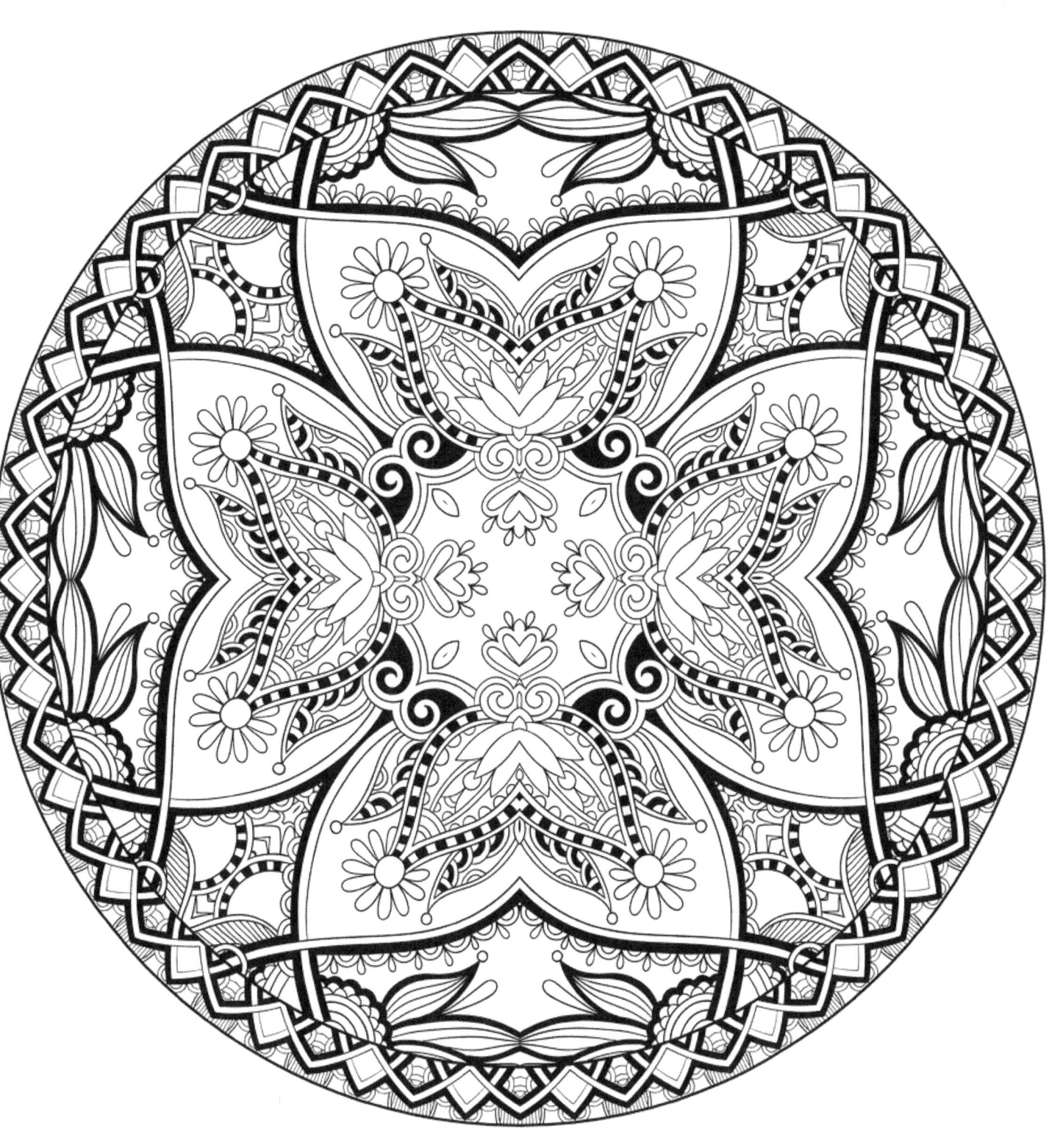

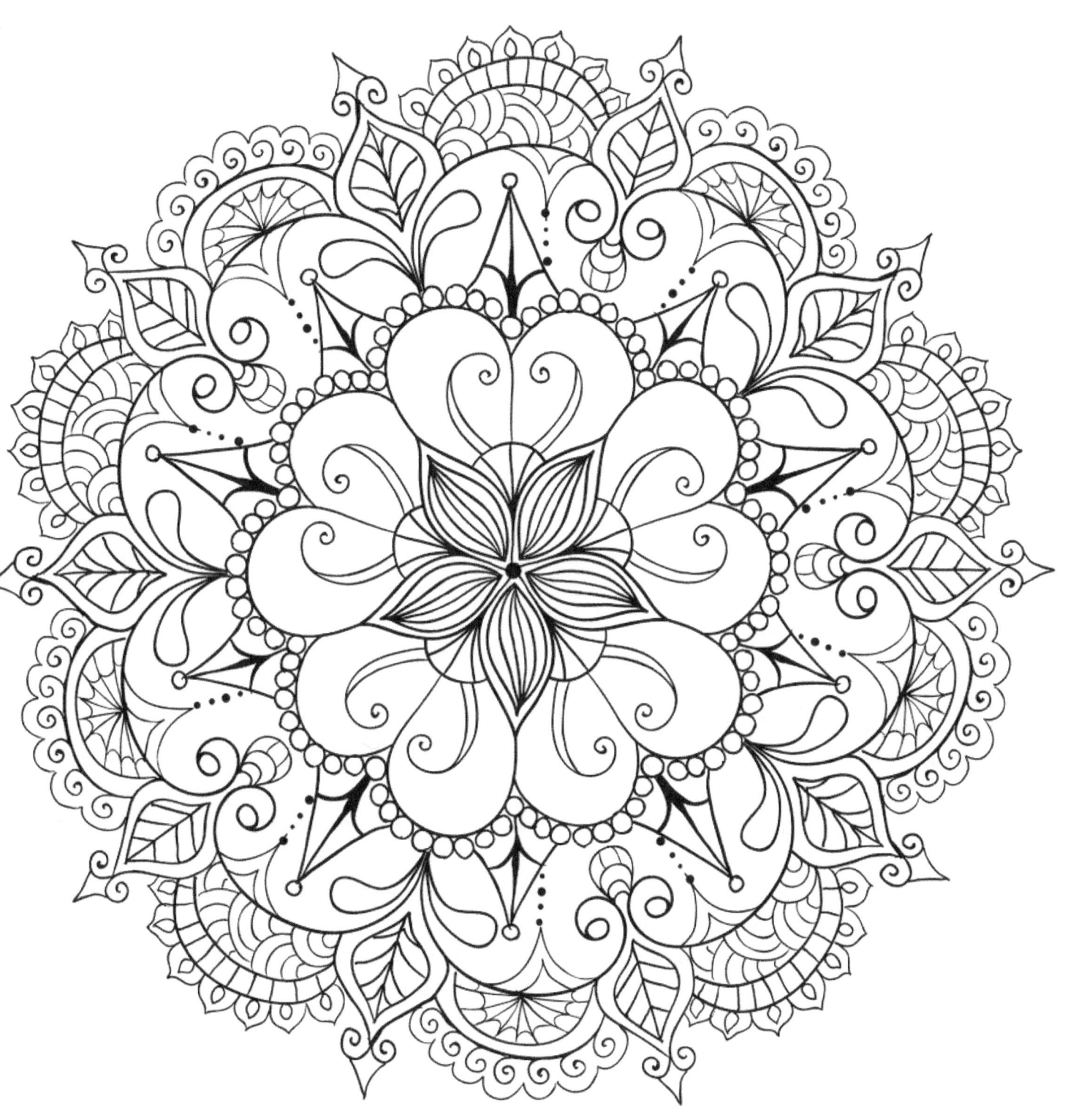

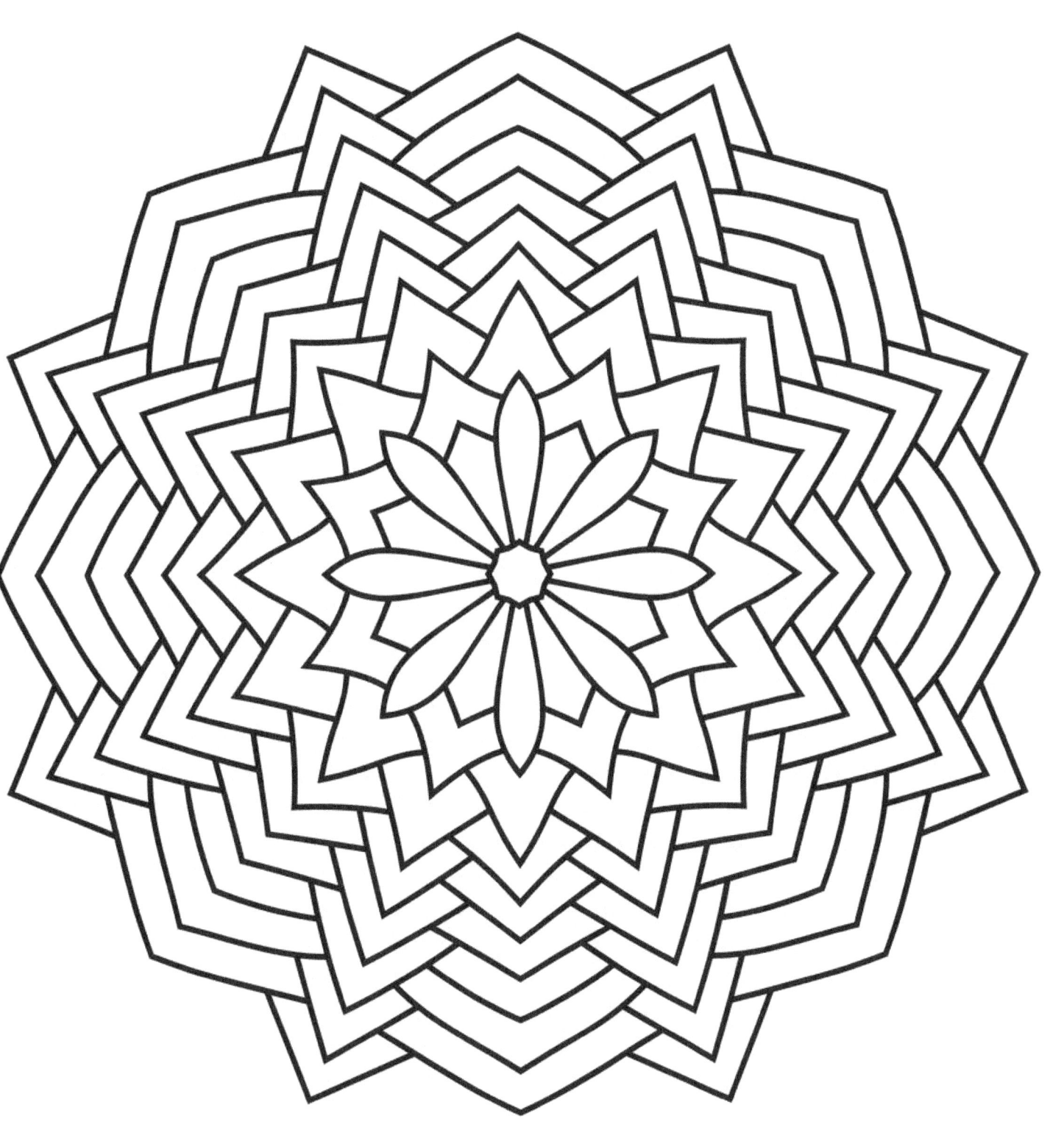

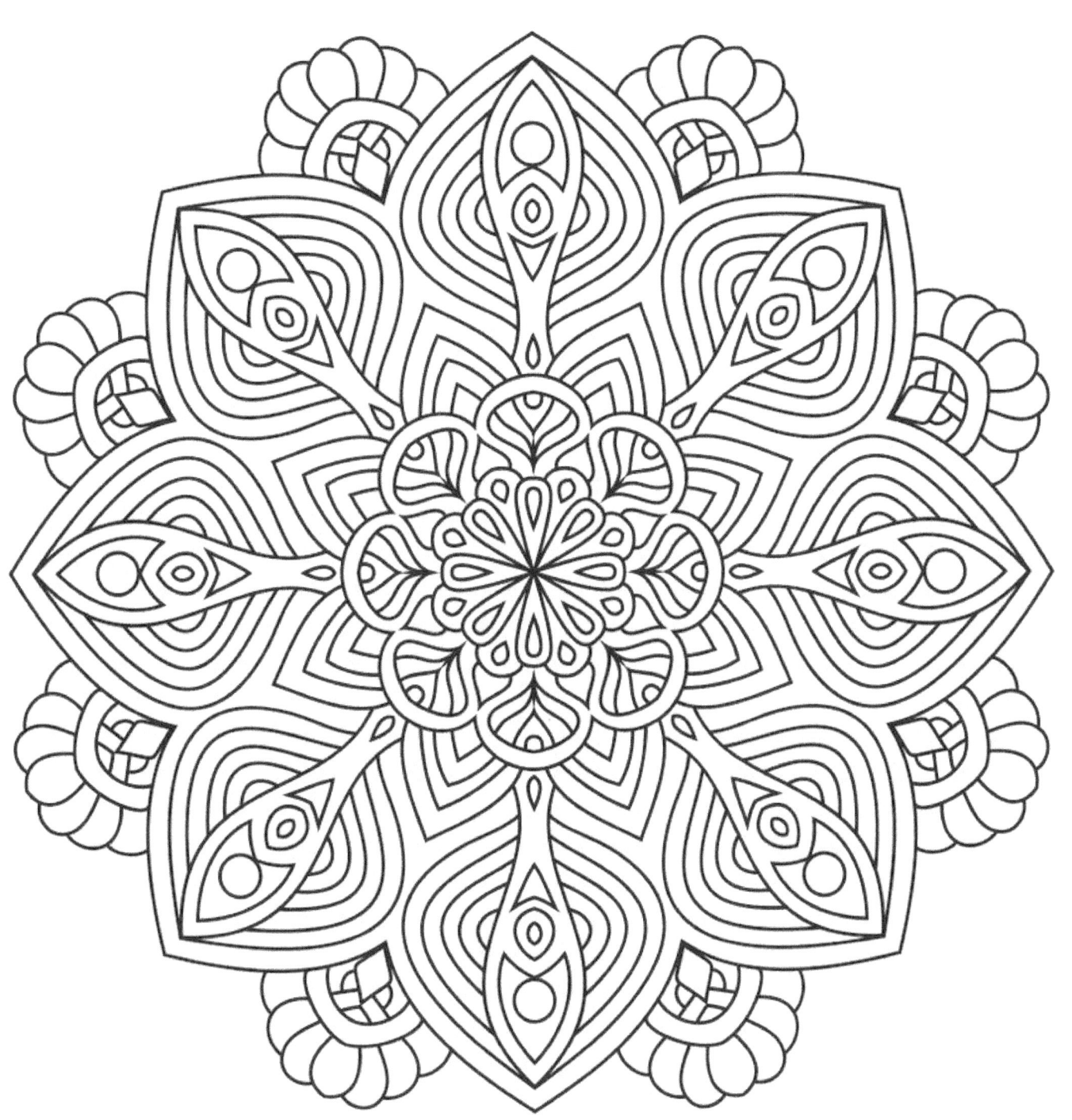

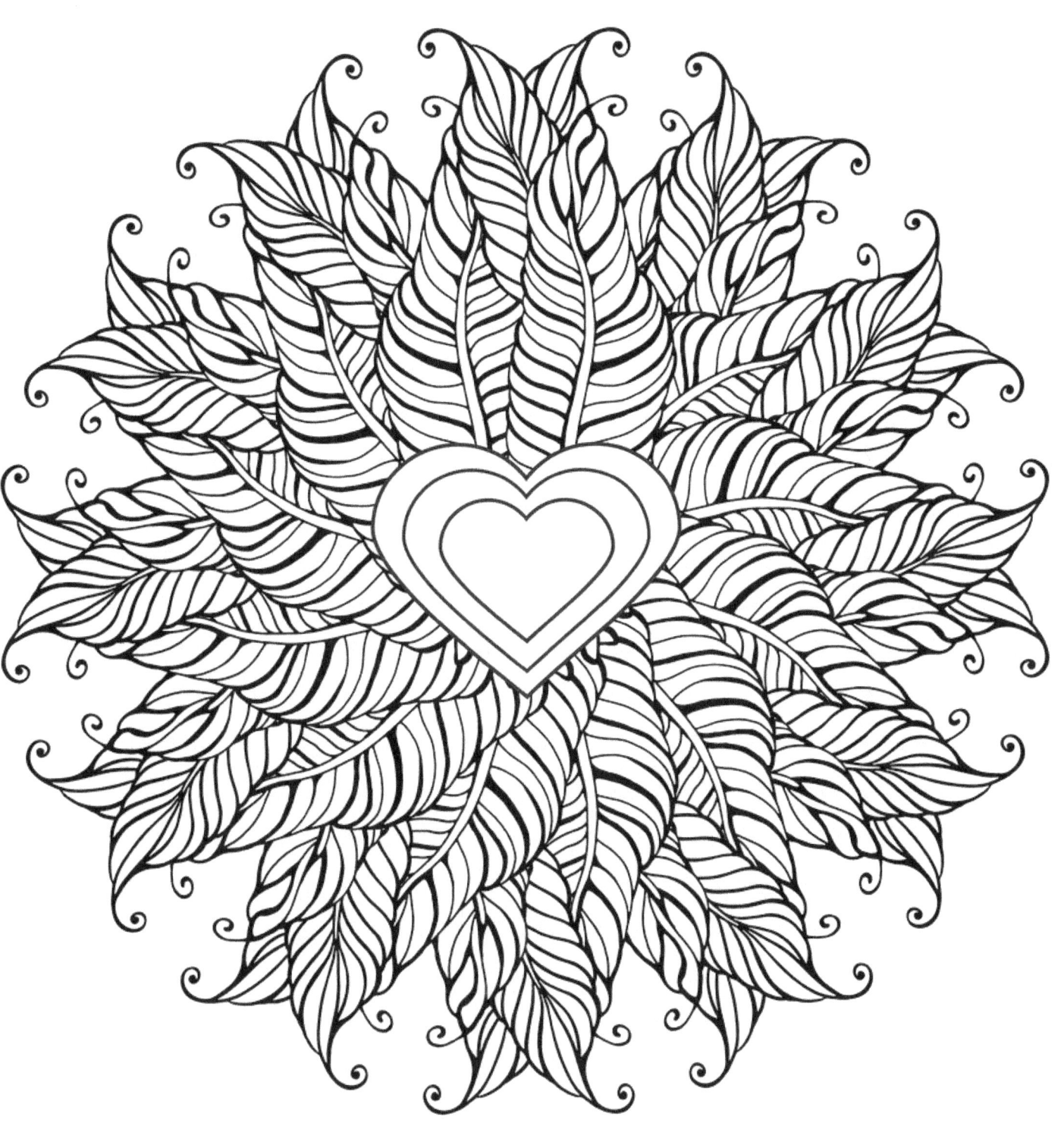

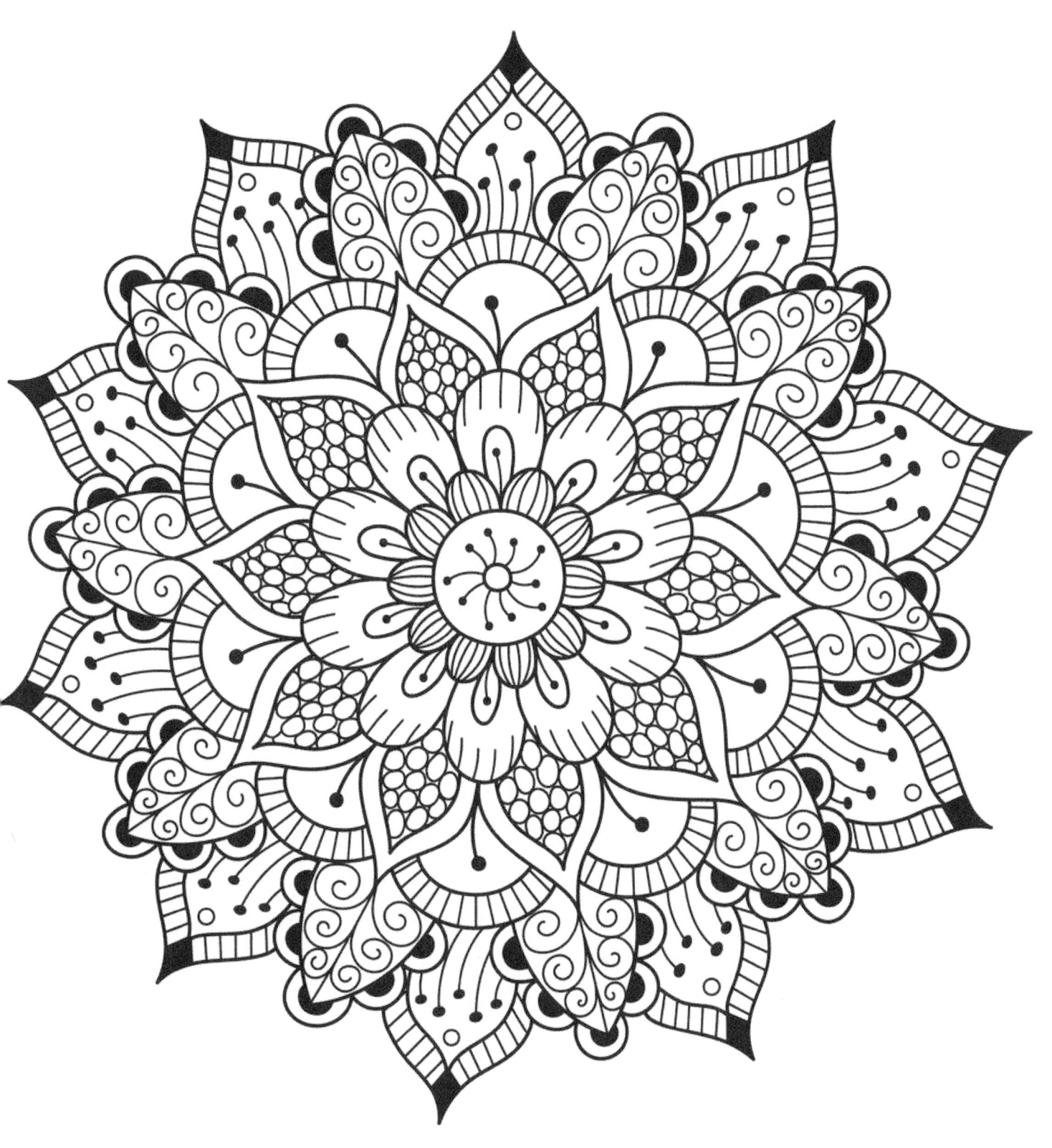

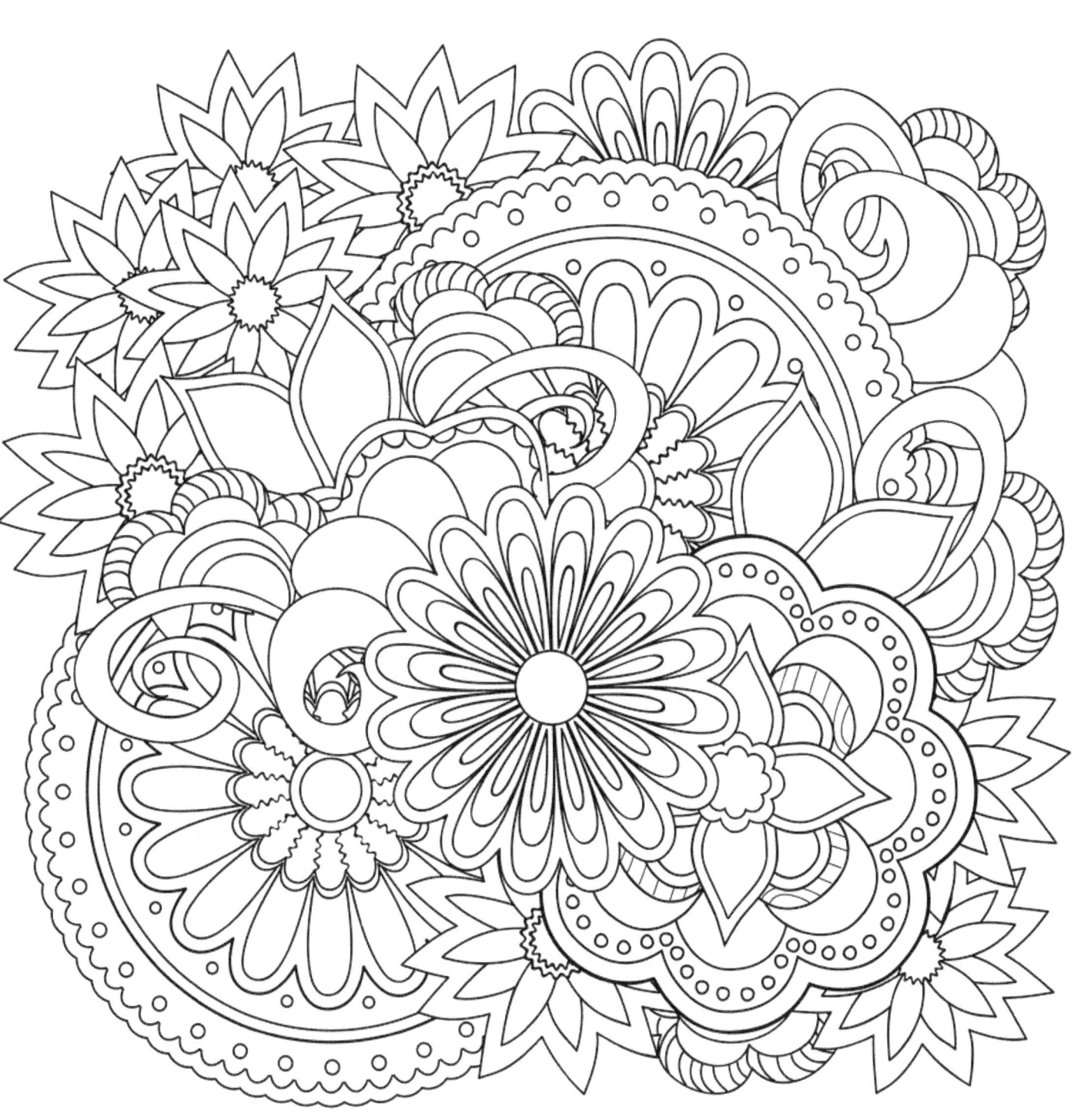

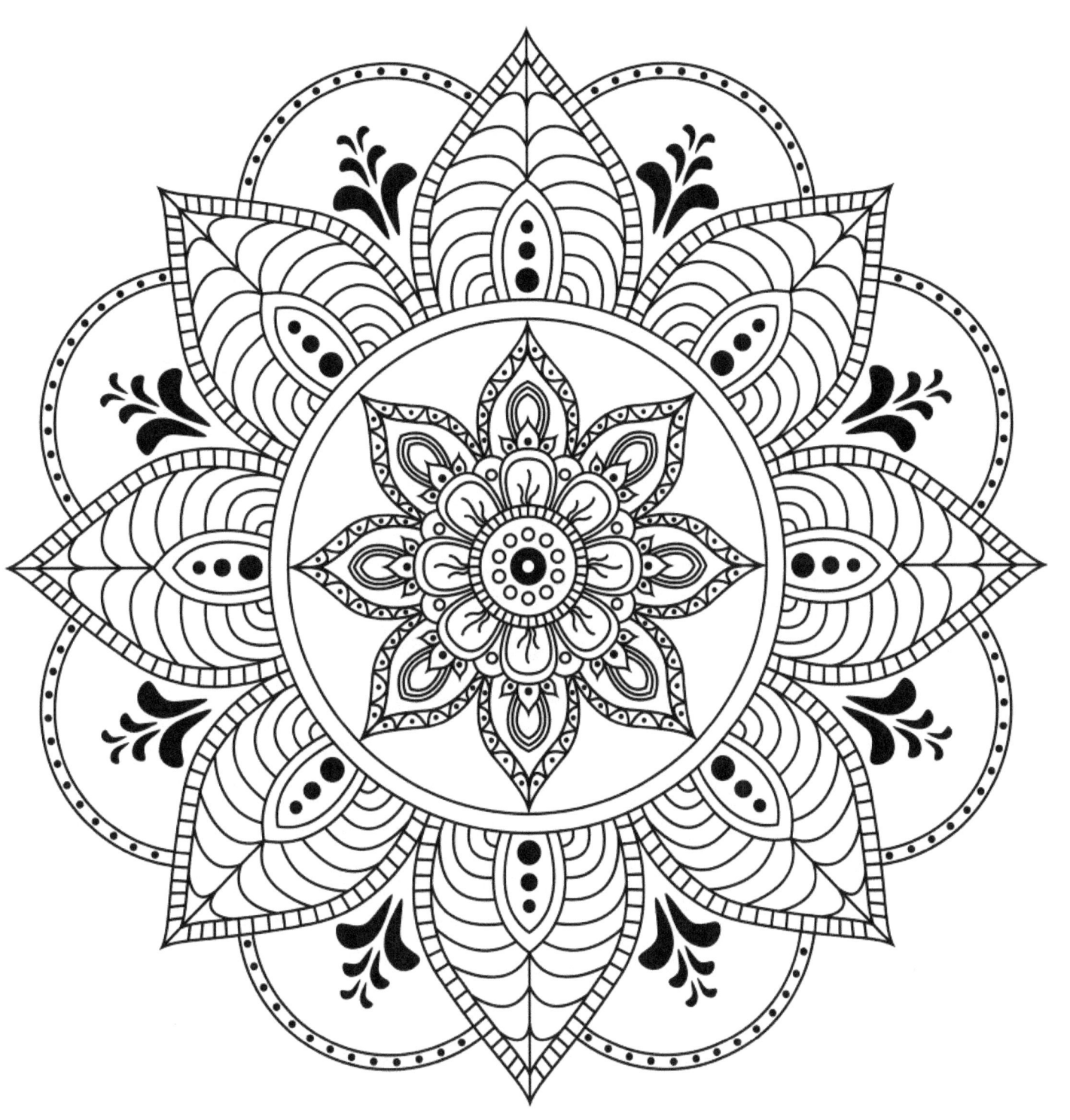

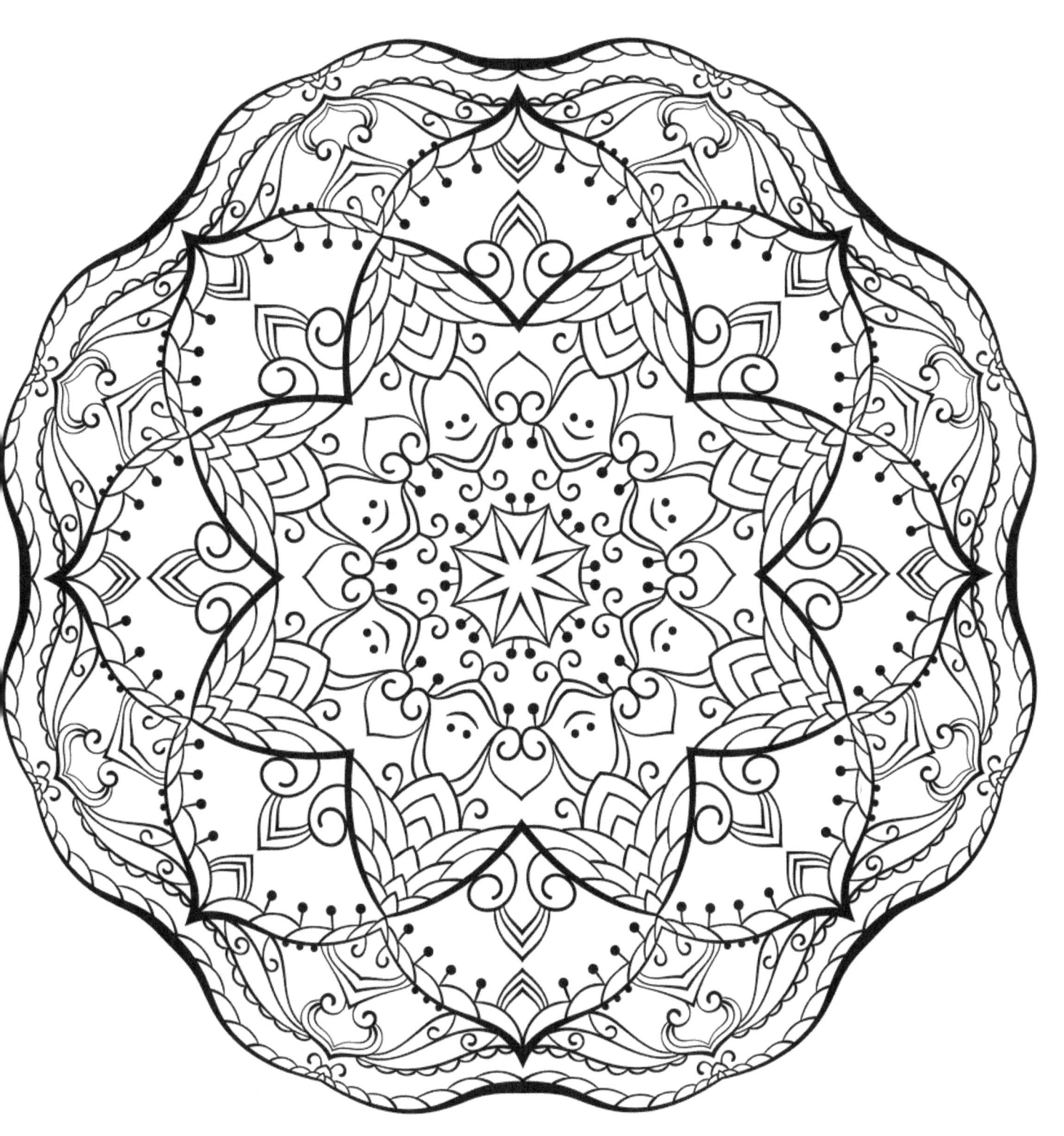

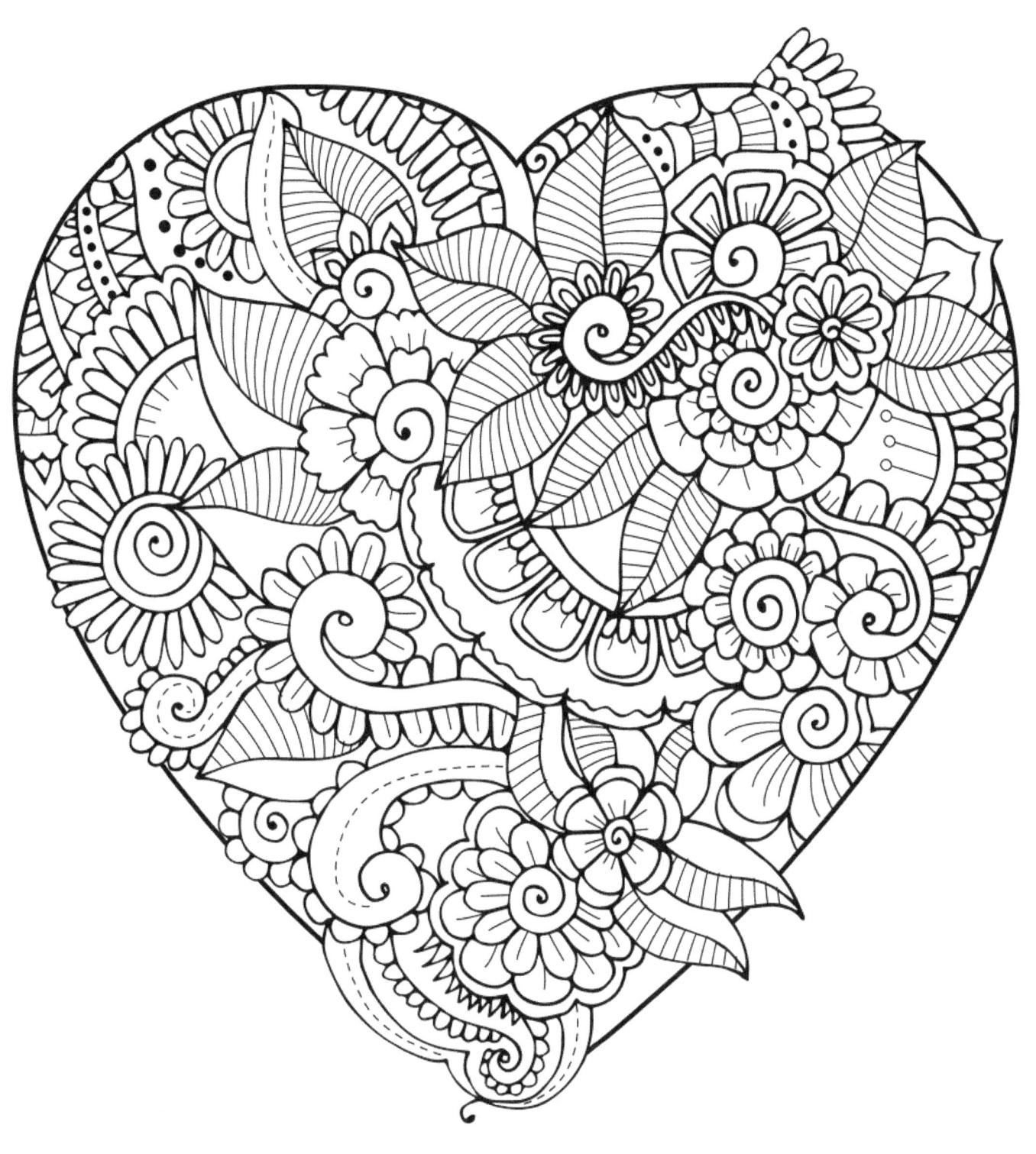

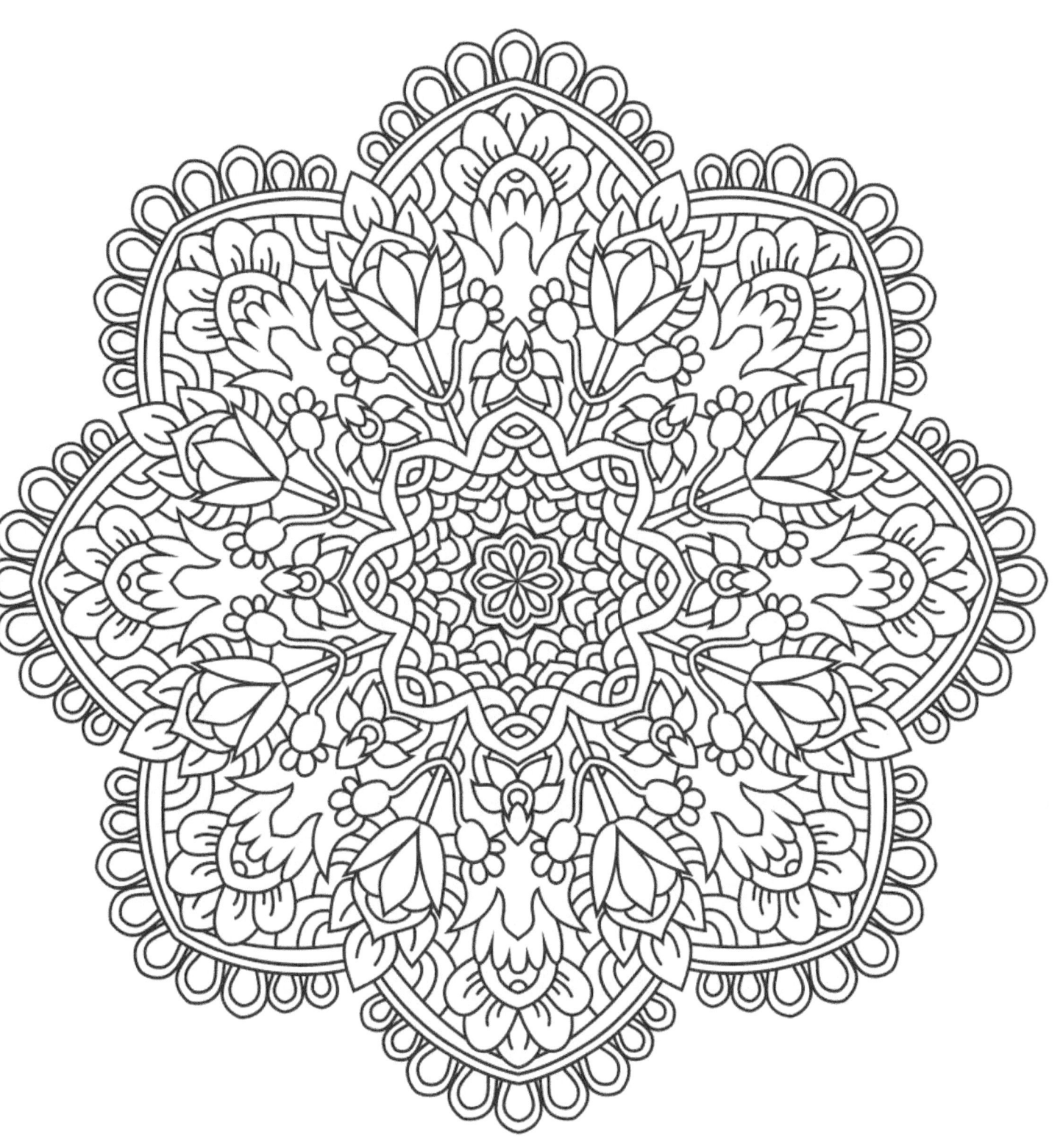

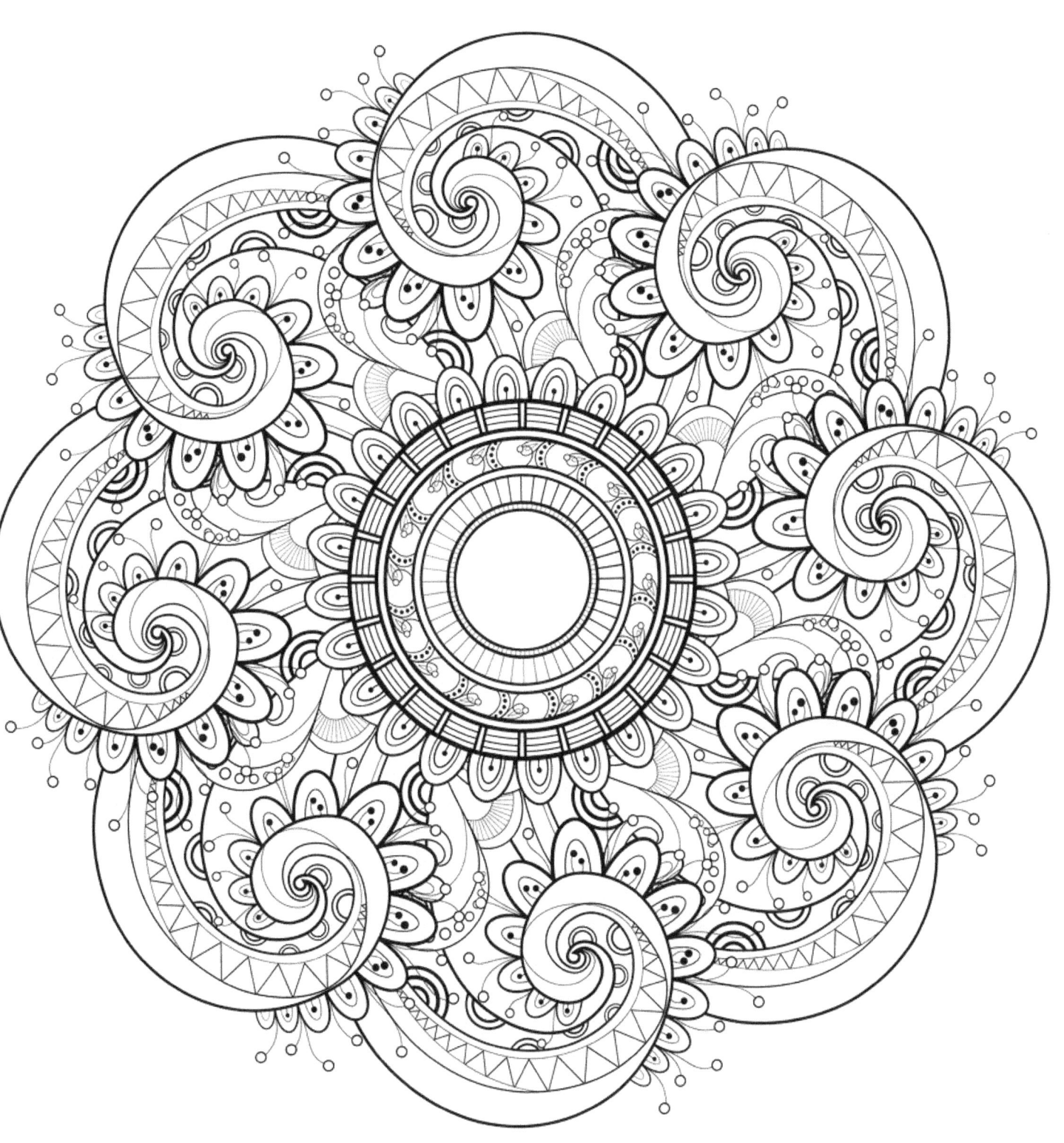

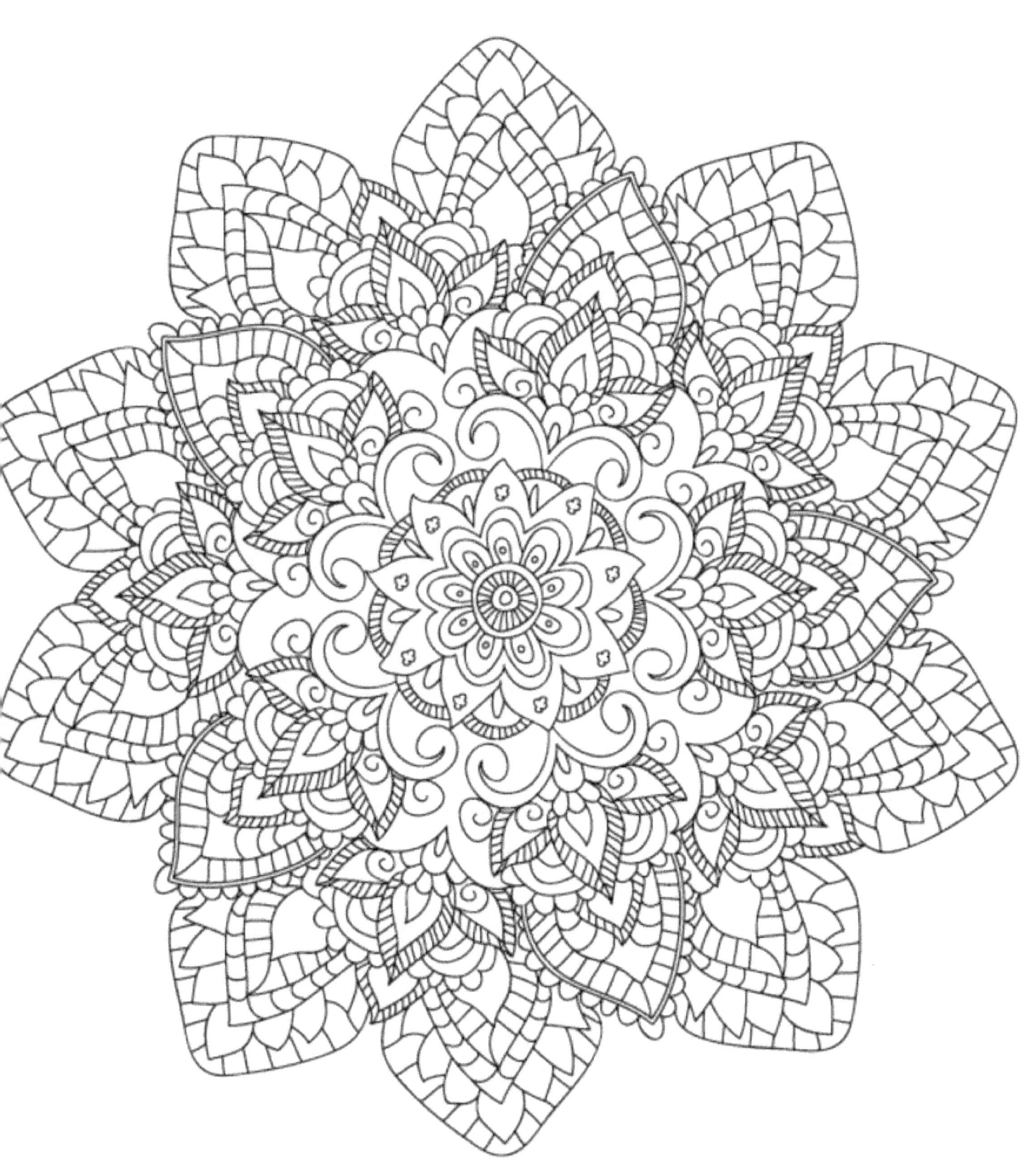

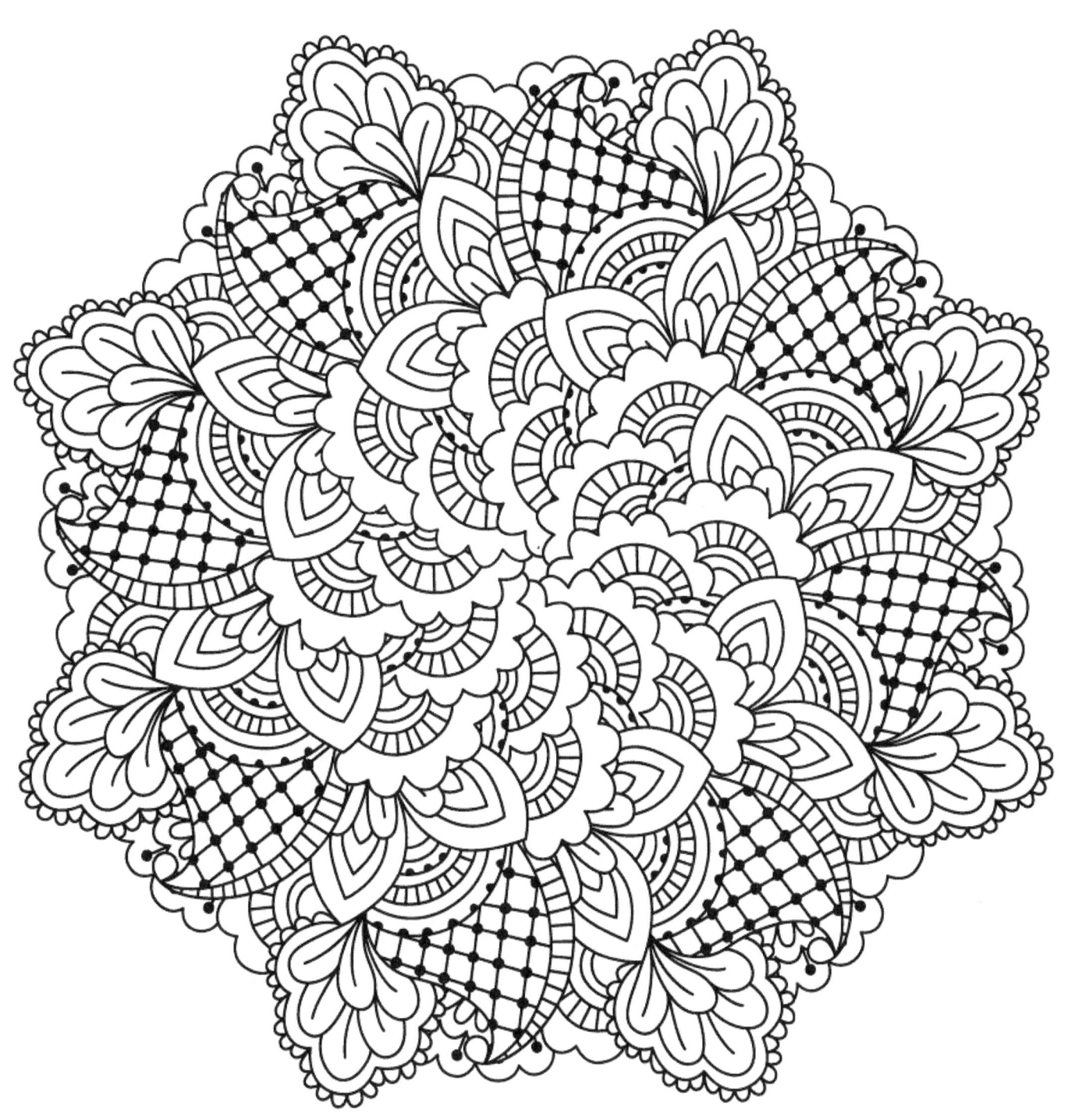

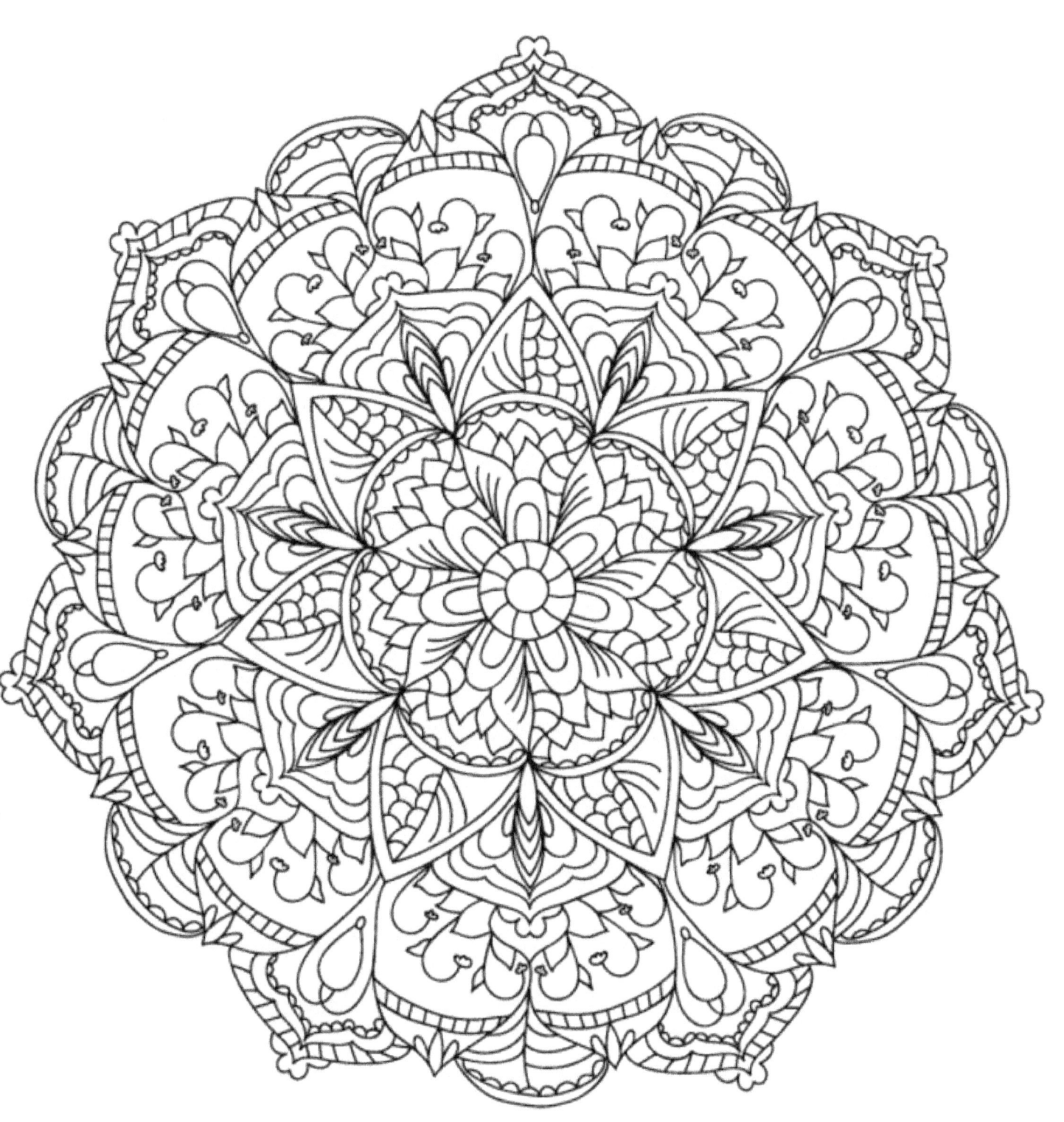

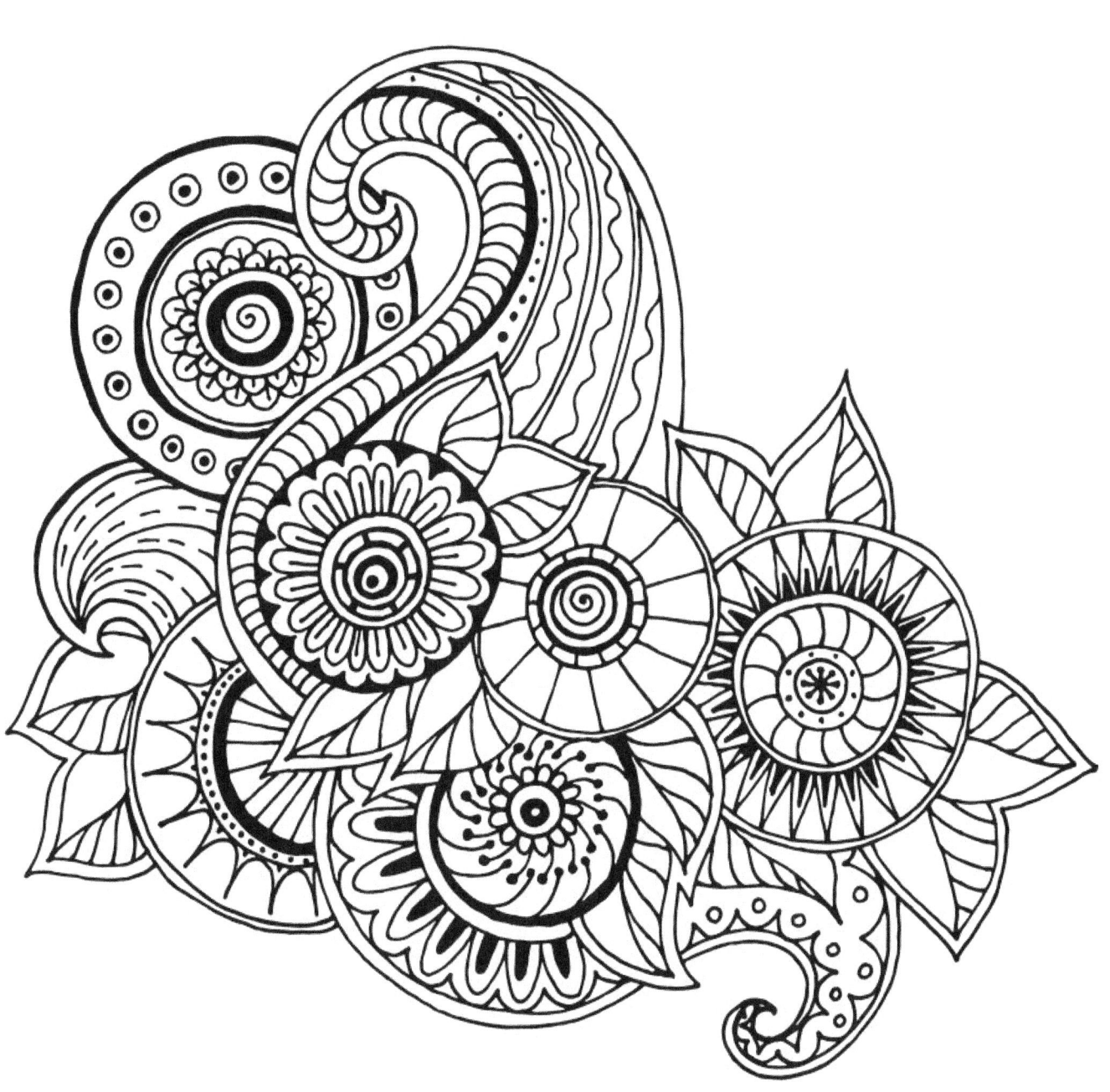

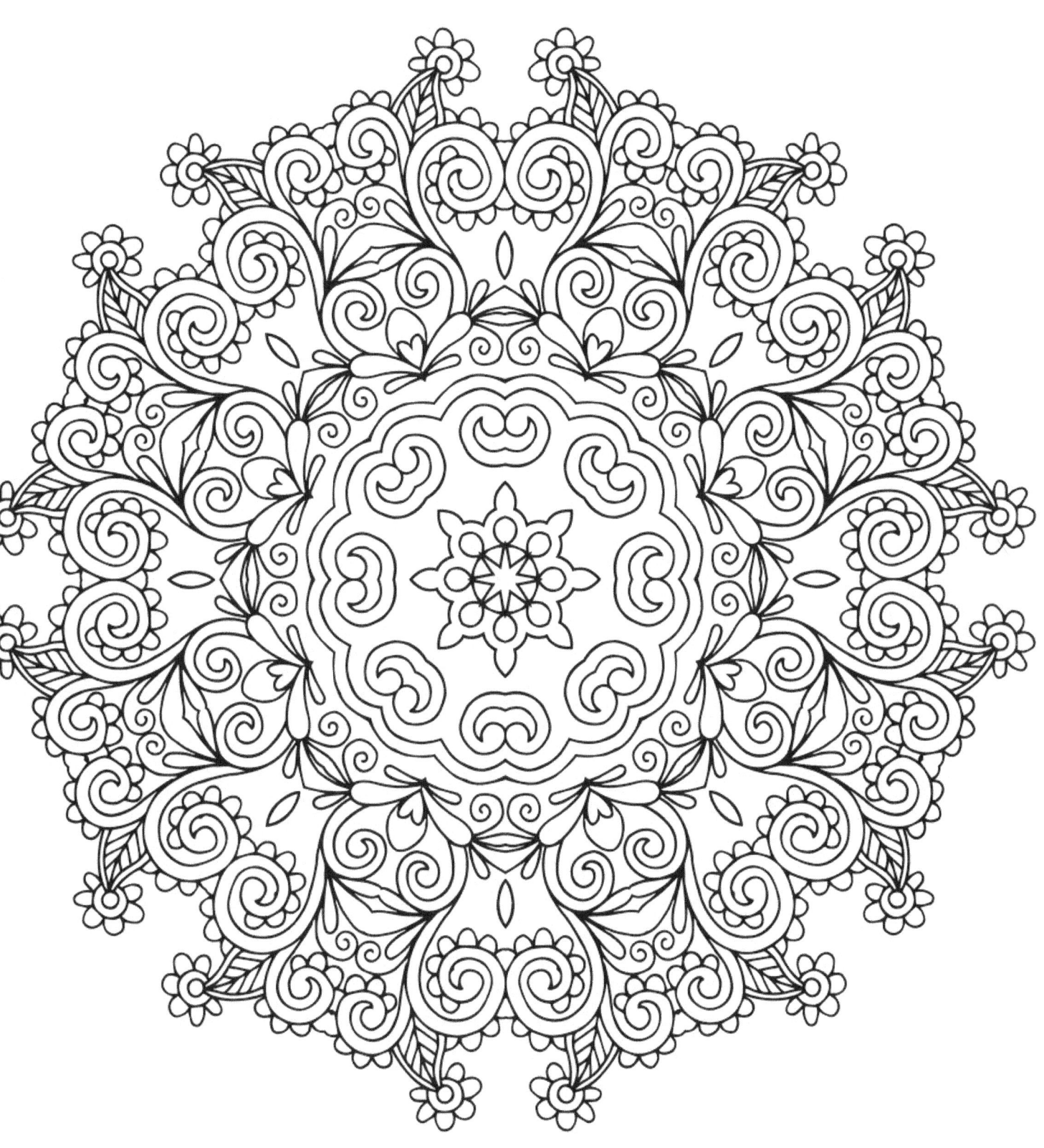

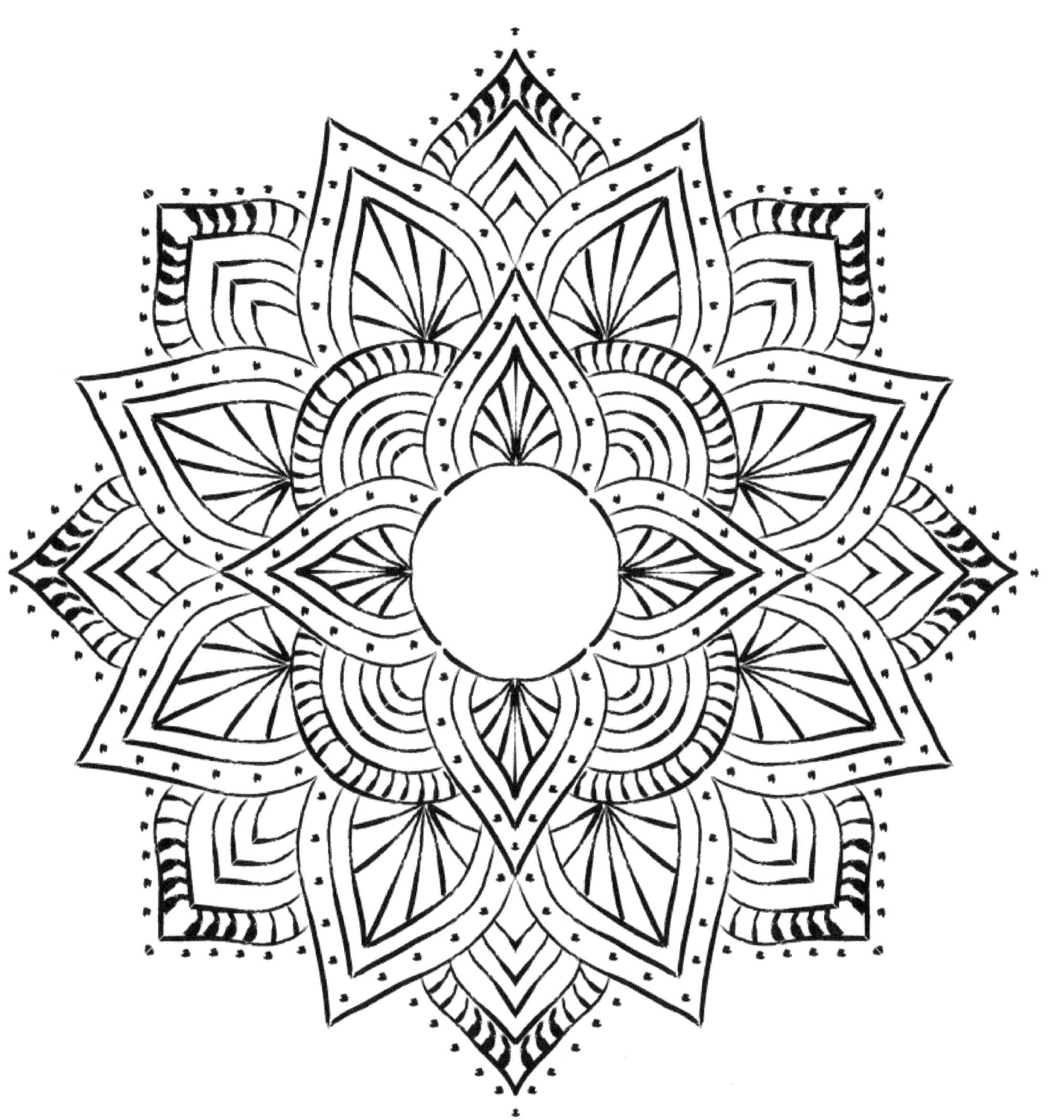

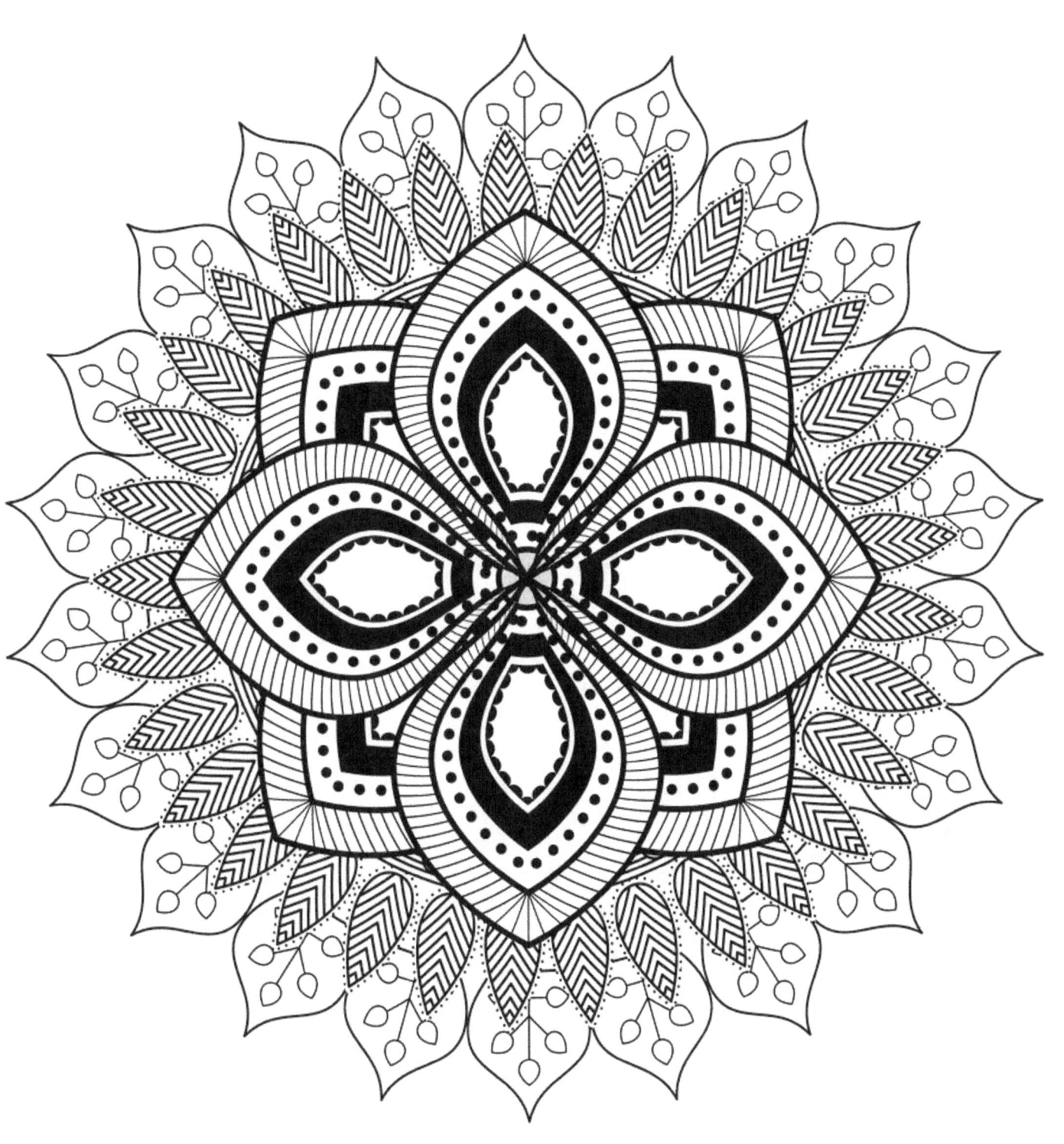

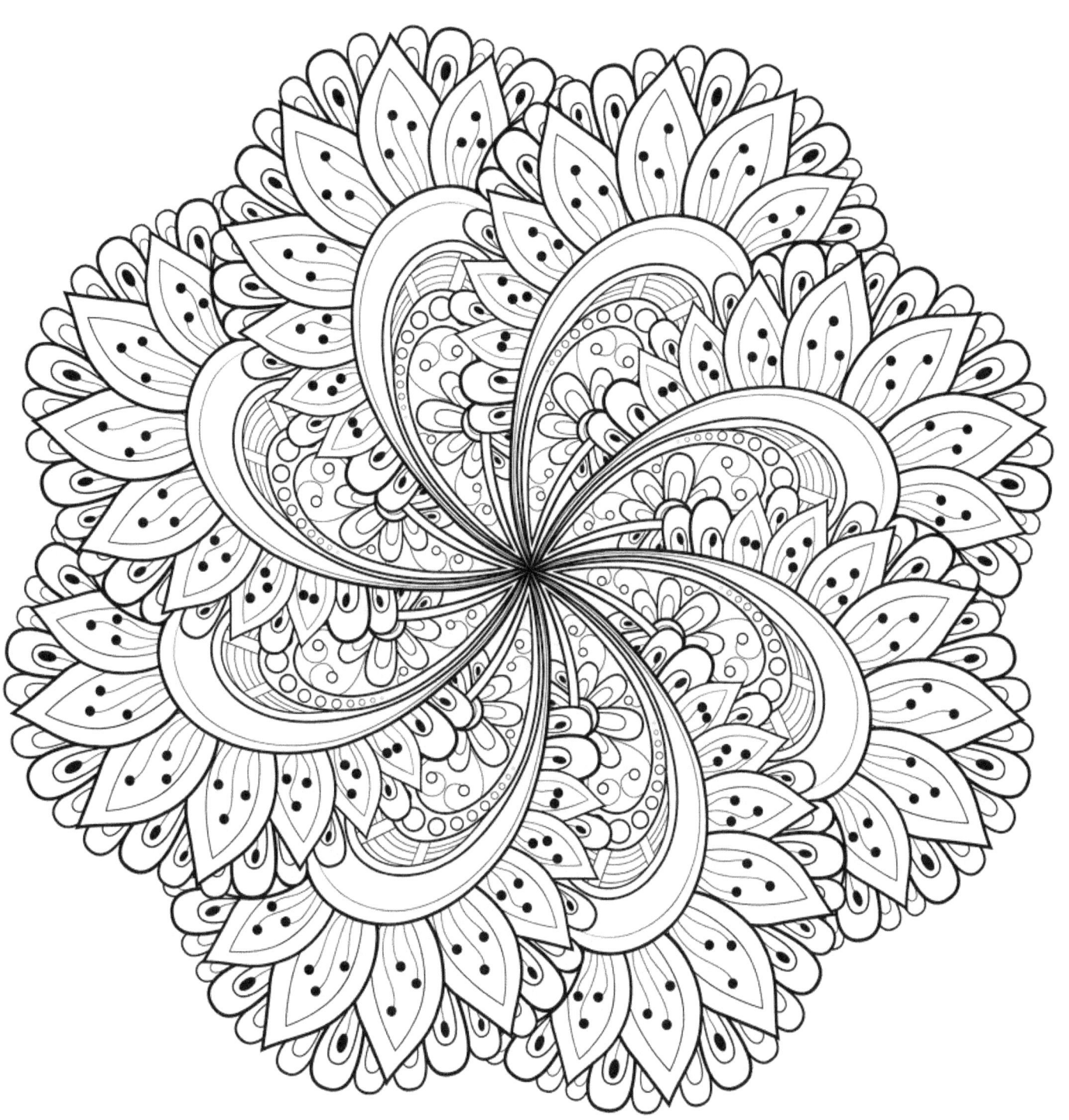

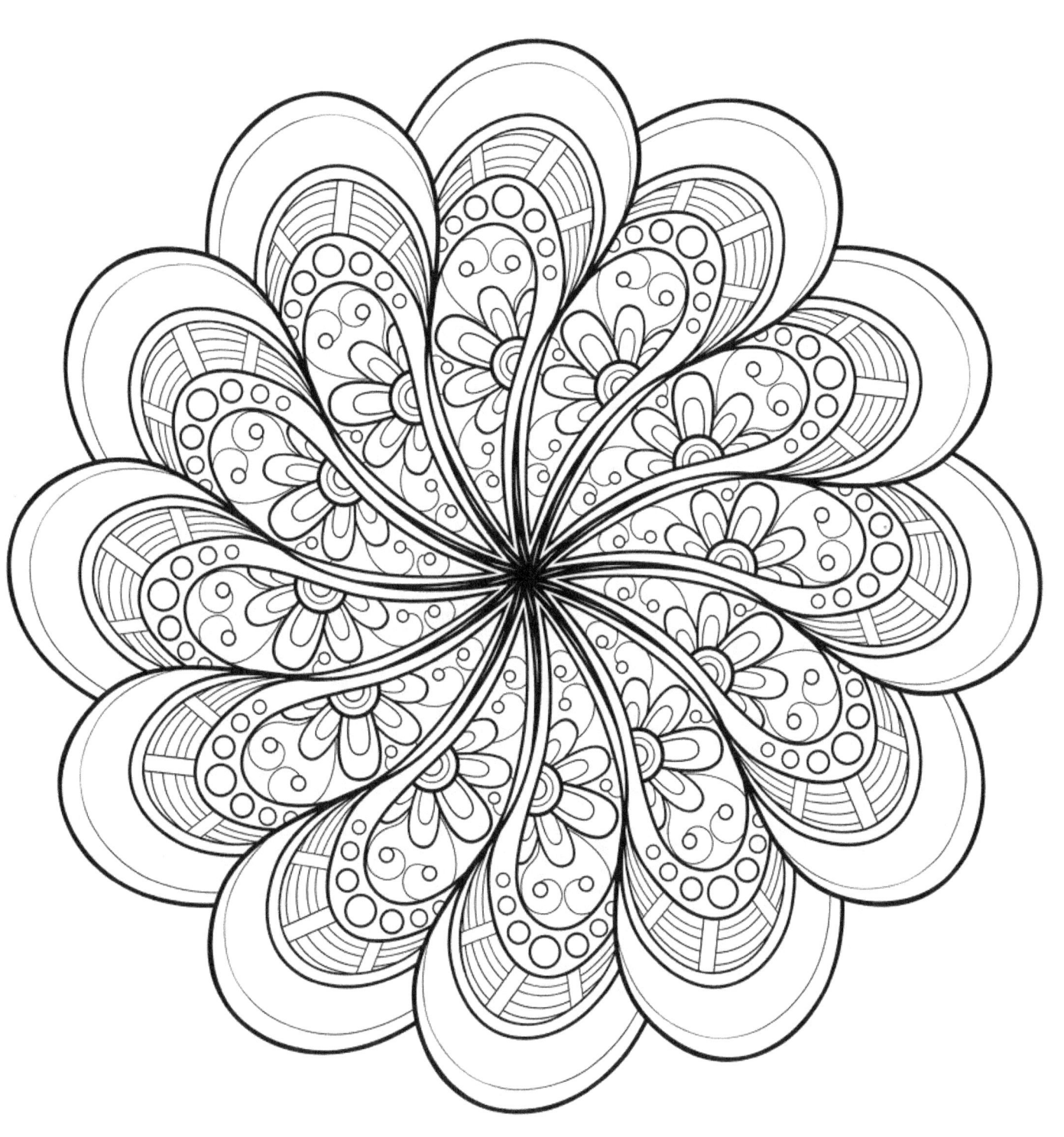

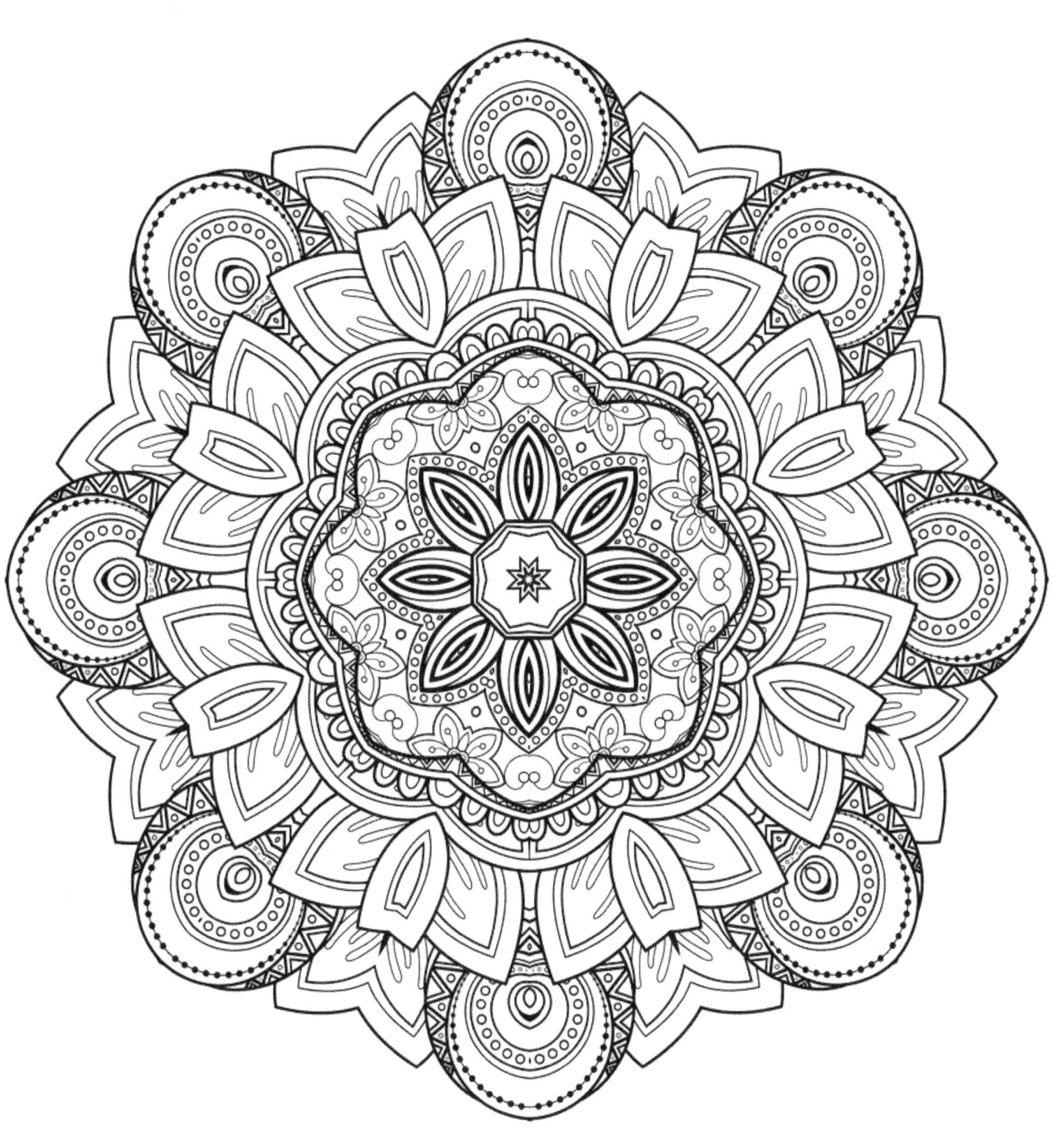

www.ingramcontent.com/pod-product-compliance
Lightning Source LLC
Chambersburg PA
CBHW060002230526
45472CB00008B/1913